CLASSIC MARQUES

Vauxhall Cars
1945-1964

ALAN EARNSHAW & ROBERT W BERRY

NOSTALGIA ROAD

First published by Transpennine Publishing
2000 with new edition 2001
This edition Nostalgia Road 2013

A CIP record for this book is available from
the British Library

ISBN 9781908 347190

Printed in Malta by Melita Press

Nostalgia Road is an imprint of
Crécy Publishing Limited
1a Ringway Trading Estate
Shadowmoss Road
Manchester M22 5LH
www.crecy.co.uk

Acknowledgements: Special thanks are offered to: John
Ankerman (Chairman Vauxhall, Bedford, Opel
Association); Peter Blincow (Vauxhall Heritage Services);
Tony Burnip (former Director of Supply, Vauxhall
Motors); Ray Cooper (Senior Restorer, Vauxhall Heritage
Centre); Nigel Griggs (Vauxhall Motors); Stuart Harris
(Vauxhall Motors); Barry Harvey (General Secretary
Vauxhall 1903-57 Owners Club); Gordon Jamieson (R G
Jamieson, Isle of Yell); Kerseys Garage (Vauxhall dealers
Penrith); SMT (Vauxhall dealers Scotland); Dennis
Sherer (Archivist, Vauxhall Motors); Peter Stone
(Vauxhall Motors); Larry Sutherland (former Vauxhall
dealer Lerwick).

Front Cover: This 1965 Vauxhall Cresta PC saloon is the
basic model as the deluxe model boasted dual
headlamps. This car featured what was called 'Coke
Bottle' styling, and this was carried on to the FD Victor,
which replaced the FC101.

Rear Cover Top: So typical of the publicity pictures
taken by Vauxhall at the time, this obviously 'posed'
view shows one of the very first PA models introduced
in October 1957. Mountain Rose was the illustrious
description given to this delicate shade of pink, and
the white wall tyres were another distinctive feature.

Rear Cover Bottom: A late 1956 view shows the last of
the E-Type Vauxhalls — the last series in which Luton
used just one body style for its different models. The
car shown is an E-Type Cresta, as distinguished by the
contrasting body flash and white wall tyres. It was
introduced in October 1956 for the 1957 market.

Contents Page: Seen at the 43rd International Motor
Show on 22 October 1957 is the Vauxhall range of cars
for 1958. From left to right we have four F Type Victors,
two PA Crestas and two PA Velox.

CONTENTS

Introduction

Following our very successful book *Ford Motor Cars 1945-64*, we now turn our attention to one of Britain's other major manufacturers, Vauxhall Motors. However, from the outset, we should point out a couple of salient points behind our reasoning in covering the particular time span given in the title. Some readers, and at least one leading motoring magazine, expressed surprise at the fact we chose to cover the period from 1945. Yet the period 1945 to 1964 covers what are really the two most significant decades in the development of the modern motorcar.

As readers will be well aware, the cessation of hostilities with Germany in 1945 saw Britain in a battered and bruised state after six years of total war. This war affected every sector of the British public, combatant and civilian alike, and it also dramatically changed the face of British motor manufacturing as well. This fact can be quite dramatically seen in the Vauxhall story, for the Luton plant became heavily involved in military vehicle and tank production during the war years. As a result car production suffered, and only 100 or so cars were produced at Luton during the period. On the other hand 5,460 Churchill tanks and almost a quarter of a million trucks were built.

Immediately after the war, the Government demanded that exports be given priority, and in the period up to October 1946, no less than 10,000 Bedford trucks were sent abroad. A few 10hp cars came out of the works in 1945, but it was not until 1946 that production properly resumed with H, I and J type cars. Thereafter Vauxhall went from strength to strength, raising the standard as they went.

What is crucial about the two decades following 1945 is the way that Vauxhall set about capturing the growing market, producing popular cars with radical new styling and features that were often well ahead of their time. As the private car-owner market expanded in the late-1950s and early-1960s, Vauxhall were poised to capture a major share. By 1959 they had built their two millionth car, and a new era dawned with the luxurious PA series with its modern trans-Atlantic styling. Yet for the average family man, upgrading from his motorcycle combination or bus travel, it was the advent of the HA Viva one-litre saloon in 1963 that made new car-ownership possible. More modern in styling than the Morris 1000, and more spacious than the BMC Mini, the Viva heralded a new approach as the era under consideration comes to a close. It was therefore an important 20-year period, and not one that anybody can dismiss lightly.

Alan Earnshaw,
Appleby,
May 2000

A batch of E-Type cars comes off the production line at Luton in the 1950s with a Cresta leading, followed by a brace of Wyverns.

From Marine Engines to Motor Cars

It may well seem odd to include in this section a picture of a Thames tugboat, and readers may well wonder if we have taken leave of our senses. Yet, what could be more appropriate to start a book on Vauxhall Cars than such a picture? It just so happens that Vauxhall, more commonly associated with Luton in Bedfordshire, owes its history to an estate on the south bank of the River Thames. This estate was granted to one Fulk le Breant, a mercenary knight who served King John.

After an unsavoury record as an enforcer for the King, in Oxfordshire and Hertfordshire, le Breant was granted the Manor of Luton as a reward. He married a widow named Margaret de Redvers, who owned land south of the Thames. They built a new estate on this land and named it Fulks Hall, which, after many years, came to be known as Vauxhall. Some six centuries after Fulk le Breant, a Scottish engineer by the name of Alexander Wilson had established an iron works at Vauxhall, where he produced engines and pumps for the growing maritime industry. Located in Wandsworth Road, the company rapidly expanded but Wilson had left the company by 1894.

A demand for new, more powerful tugs on the Thames in the latter part of the 19th century threatened Vauxhall's traditional business as the internal combustion engine developed, and began to supplant the smaller marine steam engines.

Financial difficulties nearly brought about the end of Vauxhall in 1896, and J H Chambers was appointed as the Official Receiver. He turned the firm around and in 1897 it became known as the Vauxhall Ironworks Company Ltd. Before the year was out, Chambers and his Chief Engineer, F W Hodges, had designed and built a petrol engine for a new launch called the *Jabberwock*, and this engine (with refinements) probably became the basis for the first Vauxhall car in 1903.

A legacy of the Fulk le Breant estate that passed down to Vauxhall is seen in the firm's famous Griffin logo, which still forms the company logo at the start of the 21st century. This mythical beast, with its composite body of a lion and an eagle, was originally used on Fulk's coat of arms, but is better known to most people as the badge that has adorned thousands of Vauxhall cars. The first of these 5hp cars had a 989cc single-cylinder engine, and was to receive very favourable reviews when it first appeared.

According to the company records, 58 of these cars were made in the cramped workshops alongside the marine engines. The purchase cost was a seemingly cheap £136. Although the 1903 model did reasonably well in reliability trials, Hodges was already looking at a more powerful 1,093cc model for 1904. A Vauxhall director, Percy Kidner, entered the car in the Glasgow to London endurance run, where it was the smallest entrant in the field. The car did surprisingly well, dropping only seven points out of a possible 100, but the event finally showed that tiller steering had no place in a modern automobile. From September 1904 onwards, Vauxhall cars had the luxury of a steering wheel.

Above: A two-seater 6hp Vauxhall was a model that had been introduced in February 1904. This is one of the early production models, as can be seen by the fact that the steering was still controlled by a tiller because, before the year was out the company changed to the more practical steering wheel. Illumination for those drivers brave enough to venture out at night was by oil lamps!

The tug *Westbourne* at Tilbury in 1891, fitted with a marine engine built by the Vauxhall & West Hydraulic Co.

In November 1904 a 12/14hp model, with a 2.4-litre engine, was introduced at a cost of £375. The company had, however, recognised that a cheaper, smaller car was needed and thus decided to design a 7/9hp model, which it intended to produce on a new seven-acre site at Luton in Bedfordshire. This move was necessitated as a result of the lack of available space in the London factory as well as the desire to have a specially built facility where motor vehicles could be constructed. The Luton works began life on 29 March 1905, and it eventually grew to occupy a 300 acre site. Meanwhile, new personnel joined the firm, and two of these would eventually make substantial contributions to its development. The first was the illustrious racing driver A J Hancock, who went on to become Vauxhall's General Manager, and Lawrence Pomeroy who would become Chief Designer. Meanwhile under the leadership of Hodges, Vauxhall made its four-cylinder car, an 18hp model with a live rear axle that cost £475 and was shown for the first time at the London Motor Show in November 1905. This was the first Vauxhall car to have flutes along the bonnet; this was a feature for which the marque would eventually become famous. The flutes were reputedly inspired by fluted edges seen on the top of an antique wardrobe.

Pomeroy was meanwhile given the task of building a 12/16hp car as a new 1906 model; this was desperately needed to replace production of the 7/9hp model that was to be phased out at the end of 1905 because it was so badly underpowered for its weight. The year 1907 was important, because the split was made with the marine engineering side of the business and Vauxhall Motors Ltd was formed. Leslie Walton became the new chairman and, along with Percy Kidner (now responsible for the engineering side of the business), he began a rapid expansion. In 1907 the development of a new car (to replace the 18hp model) commenced, and a new 2.5-litre 20hp car was produced. With an almost equal bore and stroke (92mm x 95mm), the car was just what the directors wanted to enter the Royal Automobile Club's prestigious 2,000-mile rally. Lasting 13 days, the rally demanded a car that would be both powerful and durable. The design was put together by Pomeroy whilst Hodges was on holiday in the Middle East, and on his return the car was put into production. Driven by Kidner in the RAC event that June it took first place, surpassing even the Rolls Royce entrant. At Brooklands in the December, Hancock declared a special version of the car to be 'hot stuff' after it became the first 20hp car to achieve 100mph.

As the A-Type, this 20hp model remained in production until 1913. The B-Type, a 16hp model, also began to attract attention as a sporting car, and then (as now) the achievements of sporting cars helped sell ordinary models. The B-Type not only completed the 1911 Russian reliability trials (without losing a single point), but it also gained four world speed records. Standard models sold well as a result. The demand for power saw the arrival of the 27hp six-cylinder B-Type, but these only sold in limited numbers, usually with limousine bodies. Its fans included the Romanoff family, the last of the Russian Tsars.

The first true sports car, the C-Type or Prince Henry, was another Pomeroy design and it was introduced in 1911. The following year saw the arrival of the D-Type, a modest 25hp car that stayed in production up to 1921. During World War 1 2,000 of these vehicles were supplied for military use, mainly as army staff cars but some carried ambulance bodies and at least one was used by the Royal Flying Corps as a 'direction tug'.

This model continued in production after the hostilities, and around 2,000 more were built before the model was discontinued. It cost a hefty £1,450. The year 1913 also saw the arrival of the 4.25-litre E-Type (30/98) at a cost of £1,675, which became one of the fastest production cars in the world. Around 600 E-Types were built, and remarkably almost a third of this number still survive today. The company was producing larger and faster cars but it was recognised that a smaller model was required to meet the changed financial circumstances of the period. In 1922 Vauxhall introduced the 14hp M-Type at a cost of £650. In 1919 Pomeroy left the company and went to work in America, but in Europe the financial aftermath of the war was to dramatically affect the future of Vauxhall!

In 1925 the sum of $2.5million saw the acquisition of the company by the American giant, General Motors. The Luton plant, thereafter, became this company's European manufacturing base. General Motors itself had been formed in 1904 after W C Durant had been asked by the investors of the Buick company to save it from financial ruin. Durant eventually hit on the idea that if the smaller companies co-operated with one another, they could more readily compete with the larger manufacturers. His idea met with little response, so he began his own acquisition of smaller car

In 1907 the 12/16 20hp model was introduced, but it still used the straight four engine that was re-rated to 2,354cc. This photo of a tonneau model (with Vauxhall's joint Managing Director W G Gardner in the rear seat) shows to good effect the half-elliptic suspension and early bonnet flutes.

This photo shows that little regard is paid to protecting the chauffeur from the weather. This 20hp car, straight from the production line, is fitted with four completely different tyres!

This shaft-drive motorcycle, first registered in May 1923, was one of six Vauxhall prototypes built in 1922. It featured a four-cylinder air-cooled engine with a bore and stroke of 67mm giving a top speed of 82mph. Note the famous flutes appear on the fuel tank!

Moving into the 1930s, we now present a series of pictures that show the changing face of British motoring. First of all we see a Vauxhall Velox saloon, based on the T-Type, which was introduced in 1930 with a 2,916cc engine. The engine was enlarged in 1931 to 3,317cc and became known as the T80 on account of the bore diameter.

This is a 1931 Vauxhall Cadet, with bodywork featuring a sliding sunroof and leather interior. It was available in the VX and VY versions, of which 5,932 and 3,759 were produced respectively.

Below: This photograph shows a 1931 Vauxhall Melton two-seat drop-head coupé. Sports car, drop-head coupé versions of many models became a common feature in the Vauxhall range of the 1930s.

producers. Inside five years he had an impressive list of over 20 firms, including Cartercar, Elmore, Oakland, Rainier, Randolph, Rapid, Reliance, and Welch. But the two most famous names were Oldsmobile and Cadillac.

Vauxhall continued very much as before, and it seemed that the GM President, A P Sloan Jnr, was content to let the British operation make its own style of car. The 25/70 S-Type was launched that year, and two years later (in 1927) the R-Type 20/60 appeared. This 2,762cc car was heavily influenced by Detroit, and was unusual in the choice of bodies that were offered by various coachbuilders. General Motors' expansion into Europe continued in 1929, when the ruined financial economy of Germany led Opel to sell off 80% of its shares (the remaining 20% were acquired in 1931). In Britain the year 1929 saw the T-Type 20/60 replace the R-Type. However, the firm was also working on a new 12hp saloon car aimed at the middle-class family market.

All the images in this book have been supplied by Vauxhall, but we make an exception to show this picture of a Vauxhall D-Type, in a two-tone grey livery, a 1937 saloon which is fairly representative of the kind of Vauxhall car in use in 1945. It is shown with Euan Jamieson on the Isle of Yell in the Shetlands in 1954. In the distance is the Isle of Unst, the most northerly part of the British Isles. *Gordon Jamieson*

Below: Here we have the 1936 DY with attractive drop-head bodywork by Martin Walter.

Unveiled at the 1930 Motor Show, the 17hp and 26hp Cadets were in a price range below £300 and thus more affordable than the larger saloons. Offered with a straight-six engine, in either 2,045cc or 3,180cc, the Cadet showed a distinct Chevrolet influence. The bodies came in a choice of tourer, two- or four-seat drop-head coupé, saloon, convertible saloon, with bodywork by Tickford and Martin Walter etc. Wire wheels were standard. A total of 5,932 VYs were built , along with 3,759 of the larger VX models. Quite impressive numbers as the car was only in production up to 1933. Another development came in 1931 when Vauxhall launched its first commercial vehicle, the Bedford two-ton truck. The entry in to that market was a real positive step forward, and in 1932 12cwt and 30cwt vans were launched. The following year an eight-cwt van and a three-ton truck were introduced.

On the car front 1933 saw the introduction of what proved to become Vauxhall's best-selling pre-war model, namely the Light Six ASY and ASX. Designating the choice of engine sizes, the ASY and ASX models shared a common 8ft 5in wheelbase. The ASY had a 1,530cc engine, the ASX was marginally bigger at 1,781cc. The purchase price of the ASY was £195, which probably explains why 23,294 models were built before it was superseded by the DY in 1935. The DX replaced the ASX at the same time, and the two new models were the first British cars with independent front suspension. Vauxhall still maintained its luxury car production of which the Big Six range offered a choice of 2.4-litre and a 3.2-litre engines. Also offered was the longer wheelbase BX and the BXL which had a 3,180cc six-cylinder engine. In 1936 the GY and GL 25hp sports car models were launched to replace the Big Six BY and BX models. The following year Vauxhall brought out a compact car to replace its old 10hp model, in the form of the 12hp I-Type. At a basic price of £169 it was a winner from day one, and when it was tested by *The Motor* magazine they wrote 'it seats 4 in comfort... exceeds 42 miles per gallon, and cannot fail to become one of the most popular cars on the British market.'

This was clearly the right approach, because Vauxhall records show that some 55,000 of these cars were eventually sold. It is also important to remember that the new Vauxhall Ten was an innovative step forward in British motoring history, as it was the first car with an integral body and chassis — monocoque — and the adoption of this technique significantly reduced the production costs although a chassis version was retained for light commercial production. This four-cylinder 1,203cc car was initially only offered as a saloon, but from 1938 you could buy a fixed-head coupé version.

By 1938 the 12hp I-Type and the 14hp J-Type were being made, along with a 5-7-cwt Bedford van. The I-Type employed a 1.4-litre power unit, whilst the J-Type had 1.8 litres. These would effectively take them up to the war years, and as we have already mentioned, car production was severely disrupted after 1939. No new development was undertaken on saloon cars during this period of national emergency, so we will resume our story of these models when we commence our story from 1945 onwards.

What is important to point out, as we conclude this brief history of Vauxhall, is its total commitment to the British motor industry. Even after General Motors acquired the firm, it retained the traditional name and its historic heraldic emblem.

Vauxhall's first unitary construction exercise came in the shape of the 94in wheelbase Model H 10/4. It was first introduced in 1937, and powered by a 1,203cc four-cylinder engine. The standard saloon remained in production until 1940 and was the first Vauxhall to feature metallic paint. The car shown here is the Coupé version that retained the separate chassis-body type of construction.

Built between 1937 and 1940, the 3.2-litre six-cylinder GL model featured dual-circuit brakes!

American influence can often be seen in the firm's development, but to the general public it is still considered as a great 'British' firm. The firm's commitment to customer quality showed in a number of new innovations, many of which were tested on the company's proving ground at Chaul End near Luton. Incorporating a modern research laboratory, it also had a large smooth test track featuring a banked turn leading to a braking straight of 1,402ft. The facilities also included sections for testing the durability of suspensions, steering and hill climbing. Over the years the company has continually aimed to achieve the highest possible standards, and this is reflected in the products being marketed at the start of the 21st century. Vauxhall has also done much to retain its share of the market against stiff competition from the Far East.

Yet Vauxhall has not ignored its history, and in 1993 it decided to improve its heritage collection facilities and opened a Heritage Centre at Griffin House, Luton, which features a collection of 57 Vauxhall and Bedford vehicles. This museum is not normally open to the public, but an open day is held each year. The superb collection of photographs contained in this book could have been lost forever, but they were actually rescued from a skip (literally at the 24th hour) and saved for posterity by Tony Burnip then Vauxhall's Director of Supply. Copies of these photographs are not available to the general public, but by releasing selected pictures for use in this series, Vauxhall has ensured that these wonderful and evocative images can be enjoyed by everyone.

Model Types

L-Type 1948-1951

As will be appreciated from the previous chapter, car production at Luton had not been high during the war years and no real development had taken place. Accordingly when the hostilities ended, all Vauxhall had to offer was its pre-war production models, comprising of the H, I and J types. Even then, most of what was produced was destined for export, and it was not until mid-1947 that things began to get easier. Around this time the government changed car taxation to a flat rate from the previous horsepower related system. This spurred Vauxhall to up-rate its 10hp engine to 12hp, and adopted the I-Type power unit for its new L-Type models. The first of these cars was launched in 1948.

Ostensibly a new series, the L-Type's body shell was actually an updated H-Type with both a new front and a new rear end. The new front followed the standard practice of car design at that time, whereby the front wing flowed into the bonnet and (although a separate construction) still gave the impression of being an integral unit. The headlamps were now built into the front of the wings, and the rear-hinged bonnet swept down to a low radiator grille that comprised six horizontal chrome slats.

The new rear end featured a protruding boot, and this gave considerably improved luggage accommodation over previous models. The boot also featured a self-supporting lid. The four doors of the L-Type, like its predecessor, were all hinged from the central pillar, thus making the two front doors front opening.

Two models were offered, the four-cylinder Wyvern and the six-cylinder Velox. A column-change three-speed gearbox, with synchromesh on the two upper gears, was fitted to both models. The 1,442cc OHV Wyvern had a bore of 69.5mm and a stroke of 95mm and was fitted with a single Zenith carburettor. For the customer requiring better performance, the 2,275cc Velox was the one to choose. It had the same bore as the Wyvern, but the stroke was slightly longer at 100mm — this gave the Velox a good 10mph more than the Wyvern's top speed of 60mph.

Opposite top: The Wyvern and the Velox had the same overall, and rather comfortable, body style. It was usually painted black, but had a smattering of chrome on the badges, headlamp bezels, radiator grille, hubcaps and along the famous Vauxhall bonnet flutes. Here we see a Velox, a car that had the period accessory of a two-band radio although the dog shows little interest!

Opposite bottom: The two vehicles shown in this picture indicate the extensive and diverse range of products produced at the Luton plant in the late 1940s. On the left we see a Vauxhall L-Type saloon and on the right a Bedford OLAD truck (one of 13 variations of the O-Type built between 1939 and 1953).

PRESSURE COOLING
RAISES BOILING POINT OF
WATER IN RADIATOR

MODERN FRONTAL
APPEARANCE WITH
DEEPLY VALANCED WINGS
AND SINGLE-PIECE BONNET
HINGED AT REAR

SEALED, PRE-FOCUS
TYPE HEADLAMP
RECESSED IN WING

2¼ LITRE 6-CYL
O.H.V. ENGINE

LARGE CAPACITY
12 VOLT BATTERY

TWIN
WIND TONE
HORNS

STEERING WHEEL
GEAR-CHANGE

SELF-PARKING
WIPERS
DRIVEN BY CABLE
FROM CAMSHAFT

ONE-PIECE
PRESSED STEEL
ROOF

ARM SLINGS IN
REAR QUARTERS

CENTRAL
ARM REST

HYDRAULIC BRAKES
WITH OVER 100
SQ. INS. LINING AREA

REAR SEAT WITH
BODY CONFORMITY
CHARACTERISTICS
FOR EXTRA COMFORT
AND HEADROOM

FULL WIDTH
BODY CONFORMITY
FRONT SEAT

ALL-STEEL, WELDED
INTEGRAL BODY FOR
MORE STRENGTH WITH
LESS WEIGHT.

DOUBLE-LOCKED
BONNET, CAN BE
LOCKED FROM
INSIDE CAR

THERMOSTATICALLY
CONTROLLED
COOLING

HEAVY SECTION
CHROMIUM PLATED
BUMPER—WITH
OVER-RIDERS (ON VELOX)

SIX-PHASE
CARBURATION
FOR ECONOMY

INDEPENDENT
FRONT WHEEL
SPRINGING

VAUXHALL
CONTROLLED
SYNCHRO-MESH
GEAR BOX. ALL
TEETH HELICAL
FOR SILENCE

VAU 648

This fascinating 'cut-away' picture from a period publicity brochure shows the new 2.2-litre Vauxhall Velox L-Type. It clearly illustrates the vital components of the car and thus forms a unique illustration for this book. The registration plate on the car (VAU 648) gives away its identity as a Vauxhall six-cylinder 1948 saloon.

Externally, both models appeared identical but on the inside the Velox was far more lavishly appointed. It was provided with leather seats, as opposed to the Wyvern's cloth upholstery. However, the Wyvern was later offered with leather seats as an optional extra at a cost of £20. The easiest way to tell the two cars apart was by the overriders fitted to the bumpers on the Velox. Another clue was the paint colour on the wheels and from a car-mad schoolboy's point of view, this was a dead giveaway; the Velox always had cream-painted wheels, whilst the Wyvern's were painted to match the body colour.

As mentioned the L-Type Wyvern and Velox shared the cabin of the H-Type, and this shows that the L-Type was really just a stop-gap model to satisfy the emerging post-war demand for new cars. Already a new series, the E-Type, was being developed but, in the interim, customers had to be satisfied. Even so, during its relatively short three-year production span, the L-Type had a few improvements. One notable change was the separate sidelights, which replaced the integral sidelight/headlamp arrangement of the earlier cars. The rear number plate was also moved from its original position just above the bumper and placed on the boot lid. A new Burman worm and peg steering box and kingpins were fitted from 1949 onwards. Another change was in the new 'Metallic-Chrome' paintwork offered in blue, grey, green or fawn.

In order to provide something new for 1948, Vauxhall took the 98in wheelbase HIY/HIX model, and gave it a completely restyled front and back end. The 1,203cc and 1,442cc engines were uprated to a 1,442cc engine on the four-cylinder Wyvern or a powerful 2,275cc on the six-cylinder Velox illustrated here.

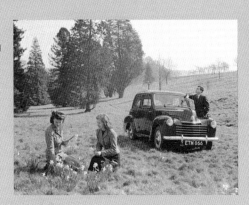

Below: This is an L-Type model, which was produced between 1948 and 1951. This particular car is the four-cylinder Wyvern, as can be identified by the body coloured wheels and the lack of over-riders on the bumper. Note the front opening front doors and the chrome trim on the bonnet.

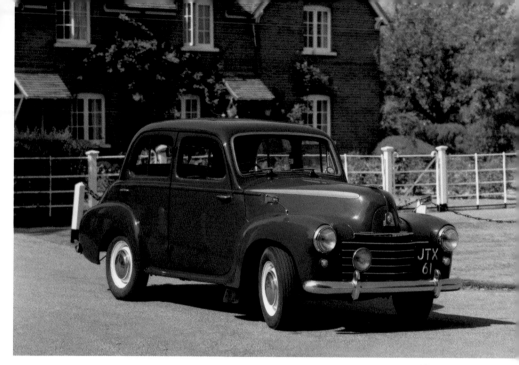

Again showing the chrome flutes, this preserved L-Type Velox, with its six-cylinder engine is taken in period surroundings that are so evocative of motoring in the immediate post-war period.

When introduced, the cars cost £447 for the Wyvern and £550 for the Velox. This actually made the Velox one of the world's cheapest six-cylinder saloon cars of the time. It was hardly a radical step forward into the brave new post-war world, but it did show indications of the new designs that were just around the corner. Already Vauxhall was gearing up for the 1950s, and it was soon 'Raising The Standard'. The dark days of the war years — which included a direct hit on the Luton plant by a German bomb that claimed 39 lives — were now firmly behind them and new and exciting Vauxhall models were just around the corner.

E-TYPE 1951-1957

Replacements for the dated L-Types were announced in August 1951, although the names Wyvern and Velox were retained for use on the new four-and six-cylinder models. The E-Type cars also initially retained the same power unit, but this was very much an interim measure as Vauxhall's new short stroke engines were in an advanced state of development. In their body shape the E-Type Vauxhalls were completely new, and the design owed much to the Chevrolet Series G Styleline that General Motors was producing in America. Using a full-width monocoque construction, the cars were to prove highly successful and 342,000 of them would be built before production finally came to an end in 1957. Both the Wyvern and the Velox shared the same body style, which featured a straight-through wing line. A curved panoramic windscreen looked out over a wide bonnet, the lid of which was side opening on the earlier

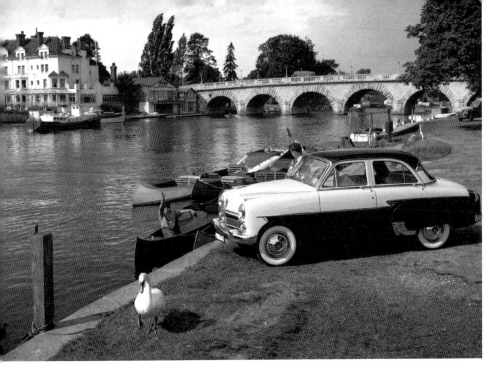

'The Car You'll Enjoy Is A Vauxhall' was the company's main advertising slogan in the mid-1950s. This publicity picture of a 2.2 Cresta was used with the slogan, and its fine lines are shown off by the eye-catching two-tone colour scheme.

models. A further feature of the bonnet was that it could be opened from either side or removed altogether for ease of access!

The E-Type's bonnet retained the famous flute on the side, whilst the Vauxhall badge was positioned on the leading edge. Below the bulbous nosed bonnet was a substantial radiator grille formed in a low, wide oval. This was divided by one horizontal bar that ran through the outer edges and ended below the headlamps, and one central vertical bar. The bumper was a relatively simple structure incorporating a slight recess. Once again the Velox had the luxury of over-riders. The top of the front wings were set level with the base of the bonnet, but they protruded out over the wheels and the wheel arches swept down in a pleasing curve that ended at the leading edge of the front doors. The sides of the car featured a mock wing line on the rear wing (which looked rather like an inverted hockey stick). Chrome-finished, push-button door handles were set just below the through bodyline.

The rear wings swept along to the tail lamps, which were contained in a chrome crescent-shaped housing situated at the top of a recess in the wings. The boot was another pleasing feature, and the sales brochures made much play about the easy loading it offered. The large, counter-balanced lid reached down almost to the rear bumper. The boot also had stowage for the spare wheel in a well below the boot floor. The rear window was much smaller than the front windscreen, and had a flat base but curved round to the roofline in a sweeping arc.

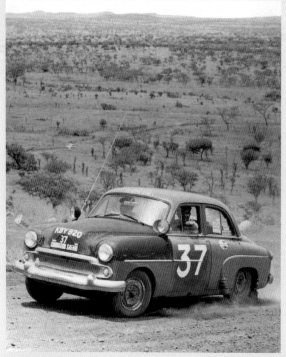

This well-known photograph has appeared in several Vauxhall brochures over the years, but it is worth repeating once again as it shows a Velox competing in the Coronation Rally in Kenya. In the 1950s the eventing and competition side of Vauxhall began to assume considerable significance and whilst never as strong as it had been in the 'Hancock days' a few people in Vauxhall saw it as a very important means of promoting sales of standard cars.

Below: A view of the Luton assembly line on 29 November 1955, showing a number of E-Type cars; first of all we see a Velox, then a Wyvern and a Cresta. Identification can be easily made by the level of exterior chrome applied to the cars. It is interesting to note that many photographs show models going 'piece-meal' down the assembly rather than being sent in blocks of one particular model. Other pictures show that light commercial vehicles would also go down the line in and amongst the cars, thus adding to the variety on the shop floor.

Identification of the different models in the E-Type series was much easier than it had been with its predecessor, as discreet chrome nameplates were situated on the leading edge of the front wings. This feature and a slightly more ornate bonnet badge on the Velox were the only real ways to distinguish quickly between the two models.

As stated, the early E-Type cars inherited their power units from their predecessors, but these developed a paltry 35bhp on the four-cylinder cars and 54bhp on the six-cylinder ones. This was clearly inadequate for the market at which Vauxhall was aiming its new models, but the problem had been clearly identified by the company and new engines were already in the design stage.

The new power units were launched in spring 1952; these had a bore diameter of 79.3mm and a stroke of 76.2mm. On the Wyvern this gave a capacity of 1,508cc, and turned it in to what Vauxhall described as a 70mph car. The Velox was now good for 80mph, and could boast a 2,262cc engine. Vauxhall favoured the 'Three on the Tree' transmission, as did Ford of Dagenham — was this a case of more Detroit influence one wonders?

Internally the car looked very handsome, and the most distinctive feature was the two-spoke steering wheel. This came in either a cream or a black finish, depending on the colour of the car's interior. The dashboard featured two circular instrument dials, one serving as a speedometer and mileage recorder, the other a temperature gauge and fuel gauge. The interior finish looked lavish, but a shortage of leather in the late 1940s had led the company to introduce a synthetic material called Vynide. The seats of both the Wyvern and the Velox used this material, as did the door panels on the Velox. The Velox interior also featured a two-tone colour scheme.

Various improvements were made to the cars during these early years, including a new facia panel in 1953. In June 1953 the bonnet saw a radical alteration, for Vauxhall changed from its side-opening arrangement to a more conventional rear-hinged bonnet. In 1954 the 'most radical improvement to the range' came with the introduction of a top-line model — the Cresta — which was launched at the Earls Court Motor Show in October that year. The new model was a Deluxe version of the six-cylinder Velox, but could be instantly recognised by its two-tone paint scheme. The division between the colours was a thin chrome strip just below the windows.

In what the company called 'trans-Atlantic styling', the car was given white wall tyres and chrome hubcaps (which featured the Griffin emblem in the centre). The Cresta logo was carried in script lettering on the lower left edge of the boot lid. A new bonnet and radiator grille were also introduced. The radiator grille was now a die-cast construction of short vertical bars, with chrome saucers at the outer ends to contain the side lamps/indicators. Above the grille ran a horizontal chrome bar, in which the Vauxhall name featured prominently.

The interior was completely revamped for the Cresta, and a new facia was provided. This had two large, recessed circular dials; one was directly in front of the driver with the speedometer, and one of an identical diameter in front of the passenger seat to take the radio speaker. Actually this was a clever piece of design planning, because the same dashboard could be used for either right-hand or left-hand drive models simply by swapping the speaker and instrument dials around. The added luxury of the Cresta warranted a two-tone (real) leather interior.

At the same time, the Wyvern and Velox models were also given a face-lift. They obtained the new facia panel, the new radiator and the new bonnet. The six-cylinder cars also obtained spats over the rear wheels. The new radiator grille did not last long, and in styling changes of October 1955, it was replaced by a chrome-plated pressing. This looked very similar to the previous design, but it was cheaper to produce and had fewer vertical bars. At this time all three models received deeper and wider front and rear windscreens. There were interior changes too, as a new roof lining material was applied. The two cheaper cars were given a new type of vinyl for their upholstery, but both six-cylinder models were given the luxury of armrest door pulls.

By 1956 the replacement models for the E-Type series were at an advanced stage of development, but it would be the following year before they were introduced. In the interim Vauxhall made yet further improvements to the E-Type models in time for the Earls Court Motor Show. Engines on these improved models benefited by the fitting of a new Zenith carburettor, whilst another improvement was the introduction of electric windscreen wipers. The 1957 cars had yet another new style radiator grille, this time one of fine horizontal bars. New tail lamps and a thin chrome waistband were new features. This band had a slight dip on the rear doors, but then rose again to follow the

In this view, we can see the spats applied to the wheels on a six-cylinder Cresta. Note how the side trim gives a suggestion of motion, and the publicity photograph taken on an aerodrome conveys an air of freedom. For those interested, the airliner is a 55-seat Boeing 377 Stratocruiser (designed in 1947) and here employed in the service of the British Overseas Aircraft Corporation.

A 1955 four-cylinder Wyvern pictured in a sylvan rural location again features in this publicity picture. Closer examination will reveal that parts of the radiator grille are finished in body colour paint; it will also be noted that the car does not feature spats around the wheel arches, although they had been applied to the six-cylinder model by this time.

rear wing line. On the Cresta a second chrome band was situated above the first, and the area between was painted a contrasting shade to the body colour. One further development in 1957 was the involvement of external coachbuilders who, with the permission of Vauxhall, produced an estate car version of the Velox. The two firms involved were Martin Walter Ltd of Cheriton Road, Folkestone and The Grosvenor Carriage Co Ltd of Kimberley Road, London.

The Grosvenor Estate had a noticeable V-shaped pillar behind the rear passenger door and a split tailgate. On this fifth door the upper half was spring-loaded and released by a press-button situated in a wide handle. The lower half of the door was released by an interior handle. The rear seat could be converted into a double bed and, like the front seats, it was covered in a soft durable material in a checked pattern. Alternatively, the rear seat could be folded away (long before the days of Flex-7 technology), leaving a large load space area finished in dark-faced plywood protected by wearing strips in polished aluminium. Grosvenor offered its conversion painted in a choice of monotone or two-tone colours. The two-tone colours were as follows: Desert Yellow with Mistral Grey; Mistral Grey/Moon Grey; Moon Grey/Mistral Grey; Bamboo Green/Mistral Grey; Mistral Grey/Apache Brown; Apache Brown/Canyon Red; and, Apache Brown/Desert Yellow. The monotone colours were: Mistral Grey; Canyon Red; Apache Brown; Bamboo Green; Desert Yellow; Moon Grey; and, Ebony Black. Some Grosvenor-bodied estates were, however, found in other colours, because in addition to modifying production line saloons, the firm would also convert existing or second-hand cars.

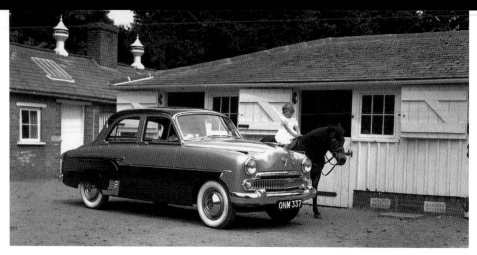

Variations on horsepower, in yet another typical publicity shot taken at a stable (the Vauxhall photographer must have liked horses as well as aircraft)! Here a young rider admires a 1956 Cresta, which may well have been painted in the popular maroon and silver straw colour scheme. The white tyre walls, chrome trim, and powerfully styled front end give a distinct 1950s trans-Atlantic look, and the American styling influences from the Chevrolet (although subtly toned down for the UK market) are clearly obvious.

The cost of this service was £230 and, whilst it was a substantial figure at the time, the *Farmer's Guardian* stated that this was: 'a reasonably affordable way to achieve all-round versatility, with a reliable vehicle offering a spacious goods compartment and two roomy passenger seats. At the weekend it converts back to a five-seat family saloon, with a reasonable compartment for the dogs, guns, etc.'

Martin Walter's well-known Dormobile (dormitory mobile) development on the Bedford chassis began here, as the estate version of the E-Type featured a folding front seat. This gave a sleeping area of 6ft 9in x 3ft 5in, not a lot of room but it offered 'the freedom to roam' (probably in more ways than one)! Externally the Martin Walter Dormobile had a one-piece tailgate made from plastic. When opened this top-hinged tailgate provided support and anchorage for the 'tent' that came with the car. When this tent was packed away, it could be stowed neatly with its alloy poles inside a cylindrical

Although the E-Type had become very popular as saloon cars, there was still a large gap in the range offered as production models. Ford had the same situation with the cars it made at Dagenham, but it had successfully got round the problem by working with outside body-builders who could convert saloon cars to estate or convertible models. Vauxhall's main association was with the Folkestone firm of Martin Walter, and here we see a view that shows the conversion that this company offered to existing Vauxhall owners. On an existing car, such as this Velox, the two-tone paint scheme split at the waist, as opposed to the sandwich effect on the new car conversions that started using cars off the production line in 1957.

Another firm offering conversions from the standard saloon was Grosvenor. This three-quarter-rear view of a Velox estate shows to good effect the split tailgate and the curious 'v-shaped' pillar.

Below: Martin Walter's new Dormobile estate car converted a production line saloon into a vehicle that offered a load carrying space, a shooting brake or even a vehicle in which one could go 'camping'. Note the Bedford CA pick-up truck conversion also by Martin Walter.

Below: A late 1956 view shows the last of the E-Type Vauxhalls — the last series in which Luton used just one body style for its different models. In March 1957 the Wyvern would be replaced by the F-Type Victor, and seven months later the PA Velox and Cresta models would replace the six-cylinder E-Types. The car shown is an E-Type Cresta, as distinguished by the contrasting body flash and white wall tyres. It was introduced in October 1956 for the 1957 market. Note the de-misting panel fitted on the rear windscreen.

container that was provided. The rear suspension was given 'stiffer' springing, resulting in a much firmer ride than the saloon. The overall weight, at 22^{1}/$_{2}$cwt, was actually slightly less than the saloon. The Dormobile cost £741 plus purchase tax of half as much again, making a price of £1,112 17s 0d for the new estate. The other interesting versions on the E-Type were built at the General Motors' Holden plant in Australia. Besides building the conventional saloon, Holden also built several other models. These included a handsome two-door convertible known as the Vagabond, a Woody Estate and a 10cwt pick-up/utility truck known as the Coupé-Utility, but better known in the outback as the Ute. The Wyvern model of the E-Type was discontinued in January 1957, at a time when Vauxhall changed its policy and decided that, rather than continue fitting four-cylinder and six-cylinder engines in the same body shell, it would produce two different body types. The Wyvern was, therefore, to be superseded by a completely new design, which was to be known as the Vauxhall Victor when introduced in March 1957. The two six-cylinder cars were destined to have a slightly longer life, and they remained in production until September 1957. At this time they too were replaced by a completely new design, but once again both six-cylinder models shared the same body shell. These were the PA Vauxhall Velox and Cresta, which were launched to an appreciative public in October 1957.

In all some 5,313 Wyverns were produced with the long-stroke engine during 1951-52, and a further 105,275 were built with the new engine between 1952 and 1957. As for the Velox, some 13,277 long-stroke engine models, and 222,019 cars with the 2,262cc engine were produced in the corresponding period. The Cresta was only ever built with the newer design of engine, but in its production life some 166,504 were built in the period from 1954 to 1957. In all a staggering total of over half a million E-Type Vauxhalls were built.

F-TYPE VICTOR 1957-1961

Just as the E-Type series Wyvern, Velox and Cresta owed much of their styling to the 1949 Chevrolet sedans, one can also see an American influence in the new F-Type Vauxhall Victor. The F-Type can be firmly linked with the 1955 Chevrolet, but it is curious that Vauxhall decided to develop a wider share of the market by using a more compact body shell on the new four-cylinder saloon. Introduced to the motoring public in March 1957, the new Victor broke fresh ground by featuring trans-Atlantic styling, featuring a wrap-round windscreen both front and rear. To allow this, the door pillars were stepped back and this gave a fully panoramic outlook for the occupants. The famous Vauxhall flutes were now 'javelin-like' on the sides of the front wing. They then tapered back along the front doors to end at a 'vanishing point' on the rear side doors. Another horizontal line ran from the base of a curiously scallop-shaped pressing in the rear doors. These features, along with the rake of the front and rear screens, and the sweep of the front wheel arch (the rear one was lower) all gave the impression of motion, a feature that can be determined even from the static picture shown opposite.

As seen from in the same photograph, the bonnet had two pronounced 'ribs', which swept down to a low, wide radiator grille that featured a honeycomb pattern. At the outer

To capture the spirit of the Victor name, publicity pictures were taken at RAF Wytan in March 1957, alongside what was then Britain's most modern 'nuclear deterrent aircraft'. This aircraft was the stylish Handley Page Victor. It was fitted with four Bristol Siddeley Sapphire 202 turbojets, and was actually the third of the RAF's new V-bombers. The prototype first flew in December 1952, but it took until February 1956 for the first production aircraft to take to the air. Even then their service life was marred by a series of engine problems until the original power units were replaced with the more powerful Rolls-Royce Conway engines.

ends of this grille were sited the side lamp/indicator lights, which were set at the same slight camber as the outer ends of the radiator grille. This gave a harmonious and stylish front-end appearance. Beneath this, the otherwise plain bumper featured two 'bullet-like' projections on the outer ends. At the rear end, the taillights were incorporated in vertical units set into the rather high wings. The wings themselves were level with the base of the rear screen, making for confident manoeuvring in reverse gear.

The actual vehicles were of unitary construction, with two longitudinal box-section members in the underbody. This provided the mounting points for the rear spring shackles and a detachable front cross-member. In turn this cross-member carried the front suspension assemblies and the front engine mounting. The rear engine mounting was carried on a cross-member that passed beneath the clutch housing, and was bolted to the box-section body-members. A transverse pressing acted as the cabin floor, and provided a mounting frame for the front seats. A second pressing gave anchorage points for the front end of the semi-elliptic rear springs (the front suspension being independent coil springs and wishbones). Further strengthening of the body was provided by a cruciform pressing between the rear wheel arches, and this both held up the rear parcel shelf and also provided support for the back of the rear seat. Although powered by a straight four-cylinder engine, which was based on the former Wyvern power unit, the Victor's engine had a number of significant improvements, including an entirely new cylinder head. Bore and stroke were 99.37mm x 76.2mm, and this gave a displacement of 1,507cc. A Zenith VN34 carburettor replaced the 30VIGH unit that had been fitted on the Wyvern.

During February 1958, Vauxhall announced the introduction of the Vauxhall Victor estate car, a unique step forward as this was the company's first 'in-house production' estate. It

This British School of Motoring Vauxhall Victor Series 1 F-Type is pictured in a period when many housewives were taking to the road with a consequent boom in motoring schools! Another of the companies who put the Victor to this use was the Enfield School of Motoring who operated a large fleet of these cars in the late 1950s.

As this June 1958 picture shows, the 100,000th Victor rolled off the Luton production line just 15 months after the launch of the car. This averaged the staggering total of 1,538 cars every week during that time.

was to feature a one-piece tailgate and a new one-piece roof panel. Where the roof panel covered the load-space area, the pressing was slightly depressed and incorporated strengthening ribs. The luggage area was now a very spacious 22cu ft, or 45cu ft if the rear seats were folded down. This was a significant improvement over the 10.5cu ft in the boot of the conventional saloon. Also in 1958 Vauxhall offered the option to have the Victor with 'Newton Drive' two-pedal automatic transmission. This was available throughout the range of four-cylinder cars at the extra cost of £25 10s 0d including Purchase Tax — quite a bargain. Whilst talking about prices we might mention that the prices of the Victor range were as follows: Basic Saloon £748 7s 0d, Super Saloon £781 7s 0d and Estate £931 7s 0d.

Five different paint colours were offered for the basic Victor: Charcoal Grey; Empress Blue; Laurel Green; Shantung Beige; and, black. The Super was produced in any of these colours, but there was also the option to have Harvest Yellow, Horizon Blue or Gypsy Red. The estate cars often supported a roof panel painted in a contrasting colour to the body shade.

After almost two years of production, the F-Type Victor was revamped. Although it was identical with the earlier version in many ways, the Series II had a smoother, cleaner shape. The scallop shape in the rear door panels had vanished, and the chrome side flutes were extended into a fine chrome band running the full length of the body to give the car a longer look.

On the Series II cars, the radiator grille was extended into a full-width unit with integral sidelight clusters. The lower front and rear wings lost their outward bulge, and a new, sleeker, wrap-round bumper was fitted. Just one central rib was seen in the bonnet pressing, and the front end also had a brand new bonnet badge. Internally new box-pleated upholstery was used on improved seats, and the same fabric also made matching door panels.

Above: We now have a trio of pictures showing Series II Victors, the first of which is taken on the M1 motorway near to its junction with the A6. In the front row we see a PADY Cresta, a Victor Series II Super Estate and Series II saloon. The picture was taken just prior to the 1959 Motor Show, and it is safe to state that it would be virtually impossible to recreate such a publicity photo today!

Right: Although it was like taking coals to Newcastle, Pontiac Motors distributed the F-Type Victor and the PA Cresta for General Motors in the USA. This Series II had its roof painted tartan, presumably for a special customer — an expatriate Scots perhaps?

Returning to the theme of great days out and happy holidays, this Vauxhall publicity picture (reputedly taken in Norfolk) shows an F Type Victor Super. The car clearly shows the continuing American influence, and this time its genesis can be traced to the 1955 Chevrolet although very much 'anglicised'.

The Vauxhall Envoy may well be a car that many readers have never heard about, and probably for good reason as this was a car made specifically for the North American market. It was based on the F-Type Victor, but there were significant differences. The side trim, radiator grille, sidelights and larger tail light clusters are all obvious features. Another variation was the Sherwood Estate, which was marketed in both Canada and the United States as a small compact family car and targeted especially at affluent families as 'the second car' for the school run or shopping trips.

A new model was added to the range at the same time, in which refinements included individual front seats upholstered in two-tone leather. The seats themselves were adjustable for height and rake to complement the standard sliding gear. This new model was the Vauxhall Victor Deluxe, and its promotional sales material hinted it was 'THE CAR' for the well-to-do middle class family.

During August 1960 even more refinements were made to the Series II range. One of the most obvious changes was the radiator grille, which now consisted of five horizontal bands. The Vauxhall name was also spelt out in letters along the leading edge

This is the British estate car version in the F-Type Victor series, this time based on the Super model in the second series. The picture was designed to show how spacious the Victor's load compartment was. With the rear seats folded down, the load space is even more spacious. The rubbing strips on the floor are also clearly evident, as is the self-supporting counter-balanced tailgate, no signs of gas struts here! Sadly only a few of the Victor estate cars have survived.

This late Series II Victor Deluxe, shows the new style radiator grille made up of fine horizontal chrome-plated bands. It has also been given a much larger rear windscreen, offering considerably better visibility. The bumpers were now of a much more conventional design than those on the earlier model, and inside a redesigned facia had been installed. In all almost a third of a million F-Types were produced, and this sales figure was undoubtedly assisted by their 'American' look which is shown to good effect in this illustration.

of the bonnet in place of the badge that had been used previously. The model's name was also shown in a chrome badge carried on the leading part of the flutes running along the car side. The headlamp hoods were also given new brightwork, by means of a fine chrome band. At the other end of the car, the most obvious change was the rear windscreen, which was now much deeper than before. Inside a new, redesigned facia panel and other improvements continued to ensure the car's popularity with the public.

The basic Victor was still available in a choice of five colours, but these were now black, Forge Blue, Silver Grey, Regency Cream and Versailles Green. A further three colours — maroon, Havana Brown and Royal Blue — were available on the Super. The Deluxe models were available in seven colours, basically those on the Super, with the exception of the Regency Cream. Mind you, you could have the Deluxe in two-tone colours at no extra cost.

Also available as a two-tone car, the estate models were supplied in Silver Grey/black, Versailles Green/Silver Grey, Forge Blue/ Silver Grey and Regency Cream/Forge Blue. The Deluxe was available in a choice of six colours, this time Silver Grey/black, Royal Blue/Forge Blue, Versailles Green/black, maroon/Silver Grey and Havana Brown/Regency Cream.

The F-Type Victor was an exceptionally popular model and, by the time it was superseded by the FB Vauxhall Victor in September 1961, a total production figure of 390,745 had been achieved. It is also important to record three of the important events that occurred at the Luton works during its production life. Firstly the work force had risen to 22,000 from the 13,000 employees in 1953. Secondly, a capital investment programme of £36 million that had commenced in 1954 had helped the company to reach an annual production figure of around 100,000 cars a year. Thirdly, as a result of the first two factors, the annual company turnover had reached £76 million by the end

In this wonderful period view we see an early Series II F-type Victor disembarking from a BKS Bristol Freighter car transporter (powered by twin piston engines) probably at Lympe airport, whilst a Bedford TJ truck belonging to Vauxhall Motors stands alongside.

Following the introduction of the F Type in 1957, Vauxhall introduced new styling changes early in 1959. These changes are shown in this preserved Vauxhall Victor, 6549 AH. Compare the bonnet, radiator grille, bumpers and rear doors of this car with the original 1957 F Type shown elsewhere in the book. This is an early Series Two Victor, as noted by the fact that the later models had a larger rear windscreen and different radiator.

In a Gypsy Red paint scheme this 1957 F-Type Victor Super clearly shows the continuation of the famous 'Vauxhall Flutes' in the chrome trim on its wings.

of the 1950s. In 1959 the Luton plant turned out its two-millionth car, itself quite a milestone, but an exceptionally important fact to note is that the plant had taken from 1905 to 1954 to make the first million cars. It made the next million inside just five years!

PA SERIES 1957-1960

The history of these cars neatly divides into two halves, and it also links neatly with the factory expansion we discussed in the last section. This expansion and improvement finally made it possible for Vauxhall to change from using just one single body shell for all the models it produced, and thus enabled the firm to produce different models for different markets. We have already described the changes for the four-cylinder car, but the six-cylinder E-Type cars remained in production after the introduction of the F-Type Victor. This led the motoring press to speculate that 'something new was in the air', and it certainly was. All was to be revealed at the 1957 Paris Motor Show, when Vauxhall unveiled its beautiful, sleek and very, very stylish six-seat saloon. It was not only radical in its body style, but the car was also completely new both bodily and mechanically.

Although being five inches longer, two inches wider and four-and-a-half inches lower than the E-Type Velox and Cresta, a certain family likeness was retained. Styling features included a substantial Triplex wrap-round front windscreen, which harmonised at the back with a three-piece rear screen that employed thin pillars that had a pressed spine incorporated into them. At the front end the really wide bonnet had its outer sides rising to the centre line of the wing, whilst the front edge curved down to the low, wide radiator grille. Below this came the bumper, the outer sections of which curved round the corners of the front wings.

The leading edge of the bonnet had the Vauxhall name spelt out in individual chrome letters, whilst chrome strips finished off the bonnet lip and formed a slight hood above the headlamps. A continuing line of chrome trim ran along the sides of the car, ending at a point on the rear wings just before the tall oval tail light units.

Clearly showing the three-piece window arrangement employed on the early Vauxhall PAs. This style, unique in Britain, was, however, employed in America on other General Motors cars such as the Oldsmobile. Another 'American' feature is seen in the rear wings, with their fin-shape incorporating the indicators in the upper tip as can be clearly identified in this view. With plain wheel hubs and no bright trim around the windows, the car shown here is obviously the PA Velox. The broad side trim, running the length of the car, identifies this as an earlier model, as later PAs had a slightly narrower section and also a one-piece rear window!

A low flute started at the rear door handle and, growing progressively, it carried along the top of the rear wing to terminate in the rear indicator unit. On the nearside, just below the rear windscreen pillar, the fuel filler cap was located and this gave access to the 10.8gall capacity tank. Between the rear wings a wide, spacious boot — with dedicated stowage for the spare wheel and tool kit — was provided. The self-supporting boot lid also carried the number plate, which was located before it dropped down to meet the body just above the bumper.

Both the cheaper Velox and the more refined Cresta shared identical mechanical specifications, and their new six-cylinder engine was a development of the four-cylinder unit in the new F-Type Victor. (The same overhead valve 2,262cc engine was also fitted into the last of the E-Type Velox and Cresta cars.) Fitted with the new Zenith 34VNT downdraught carburettor, it had a 79.4mm x 76.2mm bore and stroke. Transmission was via a three-speed gearbox, with synchromesh on all forward gears, and controlled by a column-mounted gear lever. A Borg & Beck eight-inch dry-plate clutch and a Hardy-Spicer propeller shaft transferred power to the hypoid bevel final drive.

In the cabin the Velox used Vynide for the upholstery and Novon for the door panels, both materials being supplied by the Leathercloth Industries division of ICI. The Cresta buyer had a choice of leather, Elastofab, or nylon and Elastofab. Standard equipment on the Velox included armrests on all four doors, a folding armrest on the rear seat, dual-tone horns, front courtesy lights operated by the doors, child-locks, interior roof lamp and speed wiper. The Cresta had all these, but it was also given a heater/defroster, screen washer, courtesy lights on all four doors, cigarette lighter, an electric clock, and a stainless steel moulding to the side windows. The Cresta also boasted a bonnet emblem, full diameter wheel discs and white wall tyres.

The Velox was offered in eight single tone colours: black; Dover White; Farina Grey; Laurel Green; Mountain Rose; Empress Blue; Gipsy Red; and, Wedgwood Blue. The same shades were available for the Cresta, plus five two-tone schemes: Laurel Green/Dover White; Farina Grey/Charcoal Grey; Empress Blue/Wedgwood Blue; Mountain Rose/Charcoal Grey; and, black/Dover White.

During 1958 one or two improvements were introduced for the 1959 models, noticeably a revision in paint colours which saw the following shades introduced: Royal Glow; Imperial Ivory; Laurel Green; Royal Blue; Haven Blue; Charcoal Grey; Silver Grey; and, black. The two-tone schemes were Royal Glow, Royal Blue, Charcoal Grey, Silver Grey and black, with Imperial Ivory as the second colour applied to the roof, boot deck and back end. In May 1959 Friary Motors of Basingstoke offered an estate car conversion to the PA Vauxhalls, and gave back seat passengers an extra 1$\frac{1}{2}$in of headroom. The load space behind was generous, but when the rear seats were not in use it extended

The prototype PA Velox estate car, built by Friary Motors of Basingstoke, appeared extensively in both Vauxhall and Friary publicity material. The badge seen above the rear door pillar was only used on the prototype and on production models the F Type Victor badge was used.

So typical of the publicity pictures taken by Vauxhall at the time, this obviously 'posed' view shows one of the very first PA models introduced in October 1957. Mountain Rose was the illustrious description given to this delicate shade of pink, and the white wall tyres were another distinctive feature. The period evening clothes are another remarkable feature of this picture, clearly showing the type of market that Vauxhall aimed this stylish model at.

to a generous 71in x 40in. Access to the load space area was by means of a one-piece, top-hinged tailgate. The spare wheel and tool kit were located beneath the platform floor, but the fuel filler had to be relocated down to the nearside rear wing. Five leaf springs were fitted, as opposed to the four springs on the saloon, and six-ply tyres also came as standard. Eight two-tone colour schemes were offered, or it also came in black. However, few of the Friary estates were built on the early PA models, as the series was completely revived in September 1959.

The 1959 prices were Velox saloon £929, Velox Friary Estate £1,222 5s, Cresta saloon £1,014 and the Cresta Friary Estate at £1,308. These early models are designated PAD for the Cresta and PAS for the Velox. Several of them have been preserved and they are often mistaken, by a modern generation, as being 'old American cars'. One shudders!

PA Series 1960-1962

By September 1959 the PA series, whilst mechanically still the same, had received a cosmetic face-lift. The split three-piece rear windscreen was gone to be replaced by a single wrap-round screen. The ribs in the roof had also gone, whilst a new radiator grille — with a gently curved top — was fitted. The chrome side strips were also replaced, this time by a narrower strip at the same height that ran down the full length of the car. Thereafter the strip would serve as the dividing point for the two-tone colour models, the roof and panels below the strip being one colour, with a second colour sandwiched between. The single tone colours for the Velox and the Cresta were maroon, Regency Cream, Royal Blue, Banff Blue. Silver Grey, Kewanee Green, Coronade Yellow and black.

You may well have heard of the 'Royal Estate', well here it is! This PADX Cresta with a Friary Estate conversion was supplied to HM Queen Elizabeth.

On the Cresta there were five two-tone schemes: maroon and Kewanee Green; Royal Blue or black with Silver Grey; and Coronade Yellow and Regency Cream. Vynide was used for upholstery on the Velox in a choice of four colours — maroon, grey, brown or blue — depending on the body shade. The Cresta could be upholstered in leather or Nylon and Elastofab.

To distinguish between the new cars and the earlier models, the chassis plates on the newer models were PADY for the Cresta and PASY on the Velox. These models were, however, only produced for around one year, as a new engine was then introduced to power the six-cylinder Vauxhalls.

A significant factor in Vauxhall's increasing sales at this time was the reduction in Purchase Tax, and as far as the improved PA cars were concerned this gave prices of £929 0s 10d for the Velox and £1,014 0s 10d on the Cresta in 1959. The following year saw the arrival of the new engine and yet another face-lift, on models now designated PASX (Velox) and PADX (Cresta). The engine was now 2,651cc, developing a maximum 113bhp, a substantial increase of 31bhp over the previous power unit.

The face-lift saw the incorporation of new sidelight units at the front, whilst new taillights incorporated the rear indicators. A new thin chrome band now ran from the apex of the wrap-round windscreen, passing down the window pillars and running below the door windows before terminating at the end of the rear wing flites. Once again this band would be used as the dividing line for the two-tone colour schemes. The upholstery on the Velox was also improved and, in addition to the Vynide, a woven Tygan Rayon material was available. An optional extra for the new six-cylinder cars was the Laycock-de-Normanville overdrive unit, which cost £63 15s. This was controlled by a switch fitted

Left: Apparently showing its proud new owners touring central London, this PADX Cresta circumnavigates Piccadilly Circus in a maroon/grey livery. This was of course another publicity shot, which may be given away by its Luton registration plate 67 CBM – this number plate also appears in another publicity picture, this time on a Bedford CA van.

Above: This rear-three-quarter view of the PADX Cresta shows to good effect the changes from the earlier model Crestas. Comparing this view with that on page 34 will demonstrate the new one-piece rear window and the taillight clusters that now incorporate the indicators.

Left: The 113bhp 2.6-litre PADX Vauxhall Cresta was aimed at a very stylish, class-conscious market, which was coming very pronounced in the late-1950s. The fact that many of the pictures in the archive show people in quite 'well-to-do' or prosperous clothing clearly indicates the type of customer that Vauxhall were seeking to attract.

to the dashboard, and operated on the second and third gears in the three-speed box.

By October 1960 Luton was turning out an automatic gearbox called Hydra-matic, which had been developed by General Motors for its new compact cars in the USA. A fluid-coupling type of transmission provided three forward ratios and reverse, and the six-position selection lever was mounted on the steering column. The extra cost for this option was a mere £170. One novel feature I recall from my uncle's Cresta was the horizontal speed indicator, which had a scale reading that changed from green to amber at 30mph and from amber to red at 60mph.

New colour schemes were once again adopted, this time the choice being black, Royal Blue, Forge Blue, Silver Grey, Versailles Green, maroon, Regency Cream, Havana Brown and Lime Yellow. Seven two-tone schemes were available on the Cresta, using the same 'sandwich idea', but with the roof colour also being applied to the outer sides of the flites.

A selection of PA Cresta estate car pictures. This PASY Velox, seen in Hampshire's Loddon Valley not far from the Friary factory, is pictured wearing the alternative two-tone colour scheme that divided at the waistline. The Cresta paint scheme was a sandwich effect, and white-wall tyres were standard, but came as an extra on the Velox.

To quote the colour options again would be getting a bit monotonous, but if anyone wants to know, please feel free to write in and ask us. The problem of keeping track of colours is even more pronounced, because in 1961 they were changed again, when the Velox could be bought in 14 different hues, whilst the Cresta had 15 monotones and nine duo-tone schemes.

At the time the second colour changes were made to the range in 1961, there were also a number of cosmetic changes as well, but the design was seen as 'dated' and, with the new FB Victor already on the market, 1962 would see the introduction of the new PB series. Nevertheless, in the interim the PA did receive some improvements, notably front disc brakes, which aided performance considerably. The car was also given 14in wiper blades and the option of single front seats. The Velox also had the luxury of fitted floor carpets front and rear, whilst the Cresta got Rayon carpeting and a wood-grain effect finish to the facia panel. Friary still provided the official estate car conversions until the PA was superseded by the PB in 1962 but, after this change, the conversions would be carried out by Martin Walter.

The next image is an excellent view of a PADX Cresta with the Friary estate conversion. This vehicle is probably in the Havana Brown and Regency Cream colour scheme, and clearly shows the repositioned fuel filler cap on the estate car. Also of note are the new design of taillights, the new style bumper and the later style of Friary badge, which is again located on the top of the rear door pillar.

In a two-tone livery of Dusk Rose and Lilac Haze, this PADX Cresta carries yet another Friary estate car conversion and is pictured in London's Covent Garden market. Like many of Vauxhall's publicity pictures, this view captures the atmosphere of the early-1960s, in what is obviously a real Victorian setting. Amidst the architecture and atmosphere, the Cresta is seen in the company of a plethora of British Road Service lorries, with a private operator AEC Mammoth Major to the fore.

FB Victor and VX4/90 1961-1964

With almost one third of a million cars produced in the FB Victor range, this 1,508cc offering from Luton promised to be a real successor to the 1957 F-Type Victor. Launched in 1961, this modest, sober family saloon was designed to appeal to a truly European audience. The gaudy American influence with wrap-round windows, flashy chrome trim and eye-catching features had gone, and the FB emerged as a relatively conventional, almost boring-looking saloon. It was in the same basic mould as the Ford Cortina that would appear a year later in 1962, and the two cars were to become fierce competitors in the years that followed.

Style-wise the new Vauxhall could easily be considered as an early example of standardised design, featuring simple, uncluttered, yet flowing lines running from the windscreen down the bonnet, to a low full-width radiator grille. The radiator grille had a slight V, and was made up from a series of horizontal chrome bars. The headlamps were positioned at the outer edges of the grille, with lozenge-shaped sidelight/indicator clusters located below.

The flanks of the car were modest and unadorned, save for the name Victor being spelt out in stylised chrome letters on the front wings near the leading edge of the front door. A convex rib ran round the wheel-arches and along the door sills. Another style line was the short convex pressing in the rear wing that led from the rear taillight cluster to a vanishing point by the rear wheel arch. The final feature formed a slight lip following the sweep of the boot that ran along the doors just below the windows and disappeared into the leading edge of the front wing. This can be readily seen in the picture below, and if you think about this styling featured you can see that it gave the impression that the famous Vauxhall 'flute' was still alive and doing well.

The new FB Victor. Again pictured on an airfield, but with somewhat of a contrast to the picture seen on page 27. Instead of using one of Britain's most modern aircraft as a backdrop, the setting this time emphasises something more traditional. Here we see one of the famous De-Havilland DH82s, which entered service in 1939 and became better known as the 'Tiger Moth' biplane. Registered G-ANFC, it is painted bright yellow, whilst the car is a Series I Vauxhall Victor FB Deluxe. Although not shown in any of the views presented, we might mention that the Series I had an oblong rear number plate, but that on the later models was square-shaped within a frame that incorporated the boot handle.

At the Albert Memorial, erected by Queen Victoria in memory of her late husband, we see one of the new Series I FB Victors. This is the Victor FBE, which was the company's designation for the Deluxe model. The basic model was the FBS, the Super was the FBD whilst the estates were FBW (Super) and FBG (Deluxe).

This is an assembly line picture of late PA Crestas and early FB Victors, showing this to be a 1962 view. Making this in the middle of what was a transitional period at Vauxhall as new models were coming on stream, and quite possibly towards the very end of the PA production.

The basic model in the new FB range was the standard saloon, which came in a choice of six monotone colours, and featured bench seats upholstered in Pewter Grey Vynide. It sold at £510 plus £234 19s 9d Purchase Tax (adding almost half as much again to the total), making a price of £744 19s 9d. However, for the luxury of a four-speed floor-change gearbox, the price cost another £17 10. If you wanted something a little bit more up-market, the Victor Super came out at £791 8s 11d (including tax). Although it was still plagued with the Vynide seating, this model was offered in a choice of five interior colours.

Externally, the buyer had a choice of 14 body colours set off by the lavish embellishment of stainless steel brightwork around the windows. Then came the Deluxe models, with their interiors furnished in leather upholstery. Mind you Vynide was still used on the seat backs, but the car was given the luxury of individual front seats. A choice of five special duo-tone colour schemes was available for the interior, and tufted rayon carpeting adorned the floor. Further 'luxury features' included a screen washer and a powerful heater. Externally the Deluxe had the same brightwork and stainless steel trim found on the Super, but it also had V badges on the wheel embellishers. The most striking feature was the range of colours, no less than 14 monotone and seven two-tone schemes. In the two-tone schemes, the roof and rear window pillars were painted a contrasting colour to the main body paint, and a very small number were supplied with an experimental black leather cloth finish. Including tax, the Deluxe cost £847 1s 5d, and once again the four-speed box was available as a £17 10s optional extra.

For the sum of £861.13s 0d, a really attractive estate car could be purchased as a factory-built model. Based on the specification of the Super saloon, the FBW estate featured a

Here we have a study of the family resemblance between the Series I FB Victor and the PB Velox in the background. This view dates from 1963 and illustrates the striking likeness between the four-cylinder and six-cylinder models that were produced at Luton at that time, yet a feature that had been missing from the Vauxhall range since 1957. Here the famous racehorse trainer (Sir) Gordon Richards sits in his Super Estate chatting with a stable-hand.

As mentioned elsewhere, the development of standard models for use in competitions had been something that Vauxhall had found to be especially useful in attracting new custom. Here the new VX4/90 demonstrates its potential in a snow-bound section of the 32nd Rallye Automobile Monte-Carlo in 1963.

45.5cu ft load space with easy access by means of a large, counter-balanced tailgate. This tailgate featured a slight inward curve on its bottom corners which, when in the closed position, allowed the tailgate to fit neatly round the rear light clusters. The load space area measured 65in by 54¼in, and featured load deck rubbing strips of a plastic material set in chrome strips. A bench seat came as standard, but individual front seats could be specified as an optional extra, and whilst these were popular few buyers opted to have the floor-mounted gearbox lever.

However, the VX4/90 was not just a rally car, and Vauxhall marketed it as a 'town and country saloon' – a role it took to like a duck to water! Seen crossing a ford in the Cotswolds, this Series II VX4/90, clearly shows the side flash that immediately identified the larger engined 1,594cc car!

Vauxhall also offered a new 'top of the range' car with the VX4/90, in which the designation VX referred to Vauxhall, the '4' meant four cylinders, and the '90' indicated the top speed. One leading classic car magazine later described this car as: 'The hot one, with twin carbs, 71bhp engine, individual front seats, servo front discs, four-on-the-floor, a different grille and colour side-flashes. Will do 90mph: plenty of noise though, and a Cortina GT will blow it away across country.' In contrasting the VX4/90 to Ford's Cortina, the writer ignores the basic marketing concept that Vauxhall was applying to its flagship car. Basically few owners would ever have really wanted a car that could achieve really high performance, but in the image conscious days of the Swinging Sixties, first impressions were what counted. Ford had found, to very good effect, what a successful rally car could mean to its sales of standard saloons in the 1950s, and the MkI and MkII Zephyr rallying successes really did have a knock-on effect for ordinary sales. Even sales of the little Ford Anglia 105E were to show a measured improvement, thanks to the car's success in competitions.

Vauxhall, acutely aware of the importance of this facet of sales, knew it had to have a 'performance' car in the range. Using a high compression engine with an aluminium cylinder head and a twin carburettor, the VX4/90 developed 15bhp more than the standard FB Victor and was rated at 1,508cc. Because of its 'sporty' image, the VX4/90 was always sold with the all-synchromesh four-speed floor-change gearbox and had the features mentioned in the review above, but it also had revised suspension, a more comfortable foam-filled upholstery, screen wash, and a rev counter for those who really wanted to show off. Externally it could be easily recognised by the different radiator grille, its 'T' shaped rear lamp clusters and the aforementioned side-flash that was also meant to convey an impression of the Vauxhall flute. Earlier models had a slight step in the flash, with the portion on the rear door and rear wings being wider than it was on the front door and wings.

The VX4/90 was obviously the most expensive model in the FB range, with a basic price of £665 plus tax at £306 0s 7d, making a total outlay of £971 0s 7d. This was a substantial sum for what was basically an image car, but it did prove to be extremely popular, although the exact production figures are not available. Improvements to the FB range of Vauxhall Victors included the introduction of a 1,594cc engine in 1963, which was basically pre-empting the introduction of the FC Victor (known as the Victor 101) a year later. The same engine change affected the VX4/90 giving it an 85bhp rating. Also in readiness for the FC range, a final rash of improvements to the FB were introduced early in 1964, at which time servo front discs, a new facia and larger clutches became available.

It is also worth mentioning that the FB series might have been developed as a rear-engined car! Consulting engineers had been extensively studying the Chevrolet Corvair, with a view to introducing this for the European market, where it would have taken on cars like Renault's Dauphine and the ubiquitous Volkswagen. In fact Vauxhall extensively tested an FB against a Beetle, and the FB came out on top in most respects. It would have taken some getting used to, and one suspects that it would not have done particularly well as an export model! Fortunately, Vauxhall decided to resist both the American and European influence and produced a very British car. Its quiet styling, and loss of the American look did not go unnoticed, but it certainly found approval from the new General Motors president John Gordon, when he visited Luton in 1959.

Before concluding with the subject of the FB Victor, it is well worth mentioning a little about the export market Vauxhall had developed. Driven by Government in the second half of the 1940s, following the 'Export or Die' campaign, Vauxhall had found itself entering new markets in its attempts to bring in that much-needed foreign currency.

Although we could only find one picture of the Envoy saloon, we did uncover this illustration of the Sherwood Estate, and we hope that you will appreciate the chance to compare this with the British offering. We know that the Sherwood sold into Canada, and as suggested in the text at least one was first registered in the Irish Republic. Does anyone know where else these cars went, if anywhere? The Vauxhall Epic, another export model, based on Vauxhall's HA Viva has proved a little elusive also, but we at least know that it went to Australia, Canada, USA, France and Belgium. As the Epic and Sherwood/Envoy were contemporaries of one another, did the FB derived cars get to the same destinations? Vauxhall's records are not clear on the subject unfortunately.

Traditional markets like the Empire (later Commonwealth) countries had long been established, but new opportunities presented themselves, and the expansion of the Luton plant (and later the new factories at Dunstable and Ellesmere Port) reflected this factor. The year 1964 saw the massive total of 342,873 Vauxhalls and Bedfords being produced, with the popular little HA Viva being a big seller. The Viva was to do exceptionally well in Canada, building on the strength of earlier imported Vauxhalls, and it had the distinction of becoming the top-selling imported car in the land of the Maple Leaf.

When co-author Alan Earnshaw was working with David Brown Tractors in the 1960s, he found that the Canadian market (except in Quebec) was very pro-British, and we could sell our tractors far more easily than the Americans could sell theirs. To an extent the same was also true with saloon cars, and Vauxhall certainly did very well despite the nearness of the General Motors plants in the USA. All of which brings us back to a variant of the FB, which was little known in Britain (although a picture of one of these cars in a right-hand version in Ireland does exist). The car concerned was the FB Envoy (saloon version) and the Sherwood (estate car). The basic difference in these two models, when compared to the Victors, was mainly styling and detail changes, and these are evident from a comparison of the pictures.

HA Viva 1963-1966

September 1963 was to see Vauxhall launch its first small saloon car in nearly 30 years, with the introduction of the Vauxhall Viva HA. The need for a small saloon was becoming essential to the Vauxhall range, at a time when the working classes were changing from public transport to private car ownership. Essentially the motorcycle combination had proved to be the entry point for the family market, but the great success of the Morris 1000, Austin A30/A35, the small Rootes Group cars and Ford's Anglia/Popular/Prefect 100E and the Anglia 105E had shown that here was a market that really could not be ignored by Vauxhall. The main problem was that Luton was already being worked to capacity, and the output on the larger cars showed no sign of diminishing. In 1955 the Bedford truck production had to be moved to a new plant at Dunstable, and this plant was also working to capacity as the millionth Bedford was produced in 1958. The following year Luton turned out the two-millionth Vauxhall, and there was literally no capacity for a small car.

To address the problem of capacity, and given the incentive of selective financial assistance, the company announced that it was to open a new plant at Hooton, near Ellesmere Port on the south side of the River Mersey. Located on the site of a former RAF base, the site offered good communications by road, rail and sea, and of course it was also in one of the Economic Development Areas. The Vauxhall Directors considered many other alternatives, but the Cheshire site won out, and it was decided that it would be the base for the manufacture of the new 'H Concept' car. Construction work began in August 1960, and the first Viva rolled off the specially-built Ellesmere Port plant in August 1964. However, the success of the small BMC and Ford saloons (especially the Mini), prompted Vauxhall to commence the production of some Viva saloons at Luton in September 1963, just in time for the forthcoming Motor Show.

The Viva HA, the reliable small saloon introduced for the 1960s 'family market'. Its success and popularity can easily be determined by the 303,738 built between 1963 and 1966.

Styling of the Vauxhall Viva (and all the firm's new cars at that time), would have begun life in the Design Department. Using sketches, mocked-up photographs (pictures of parts of vehicles superimposed onto drawings) and clay models such as the one shown here, and a new car slowly comes to life.

Moving on from the clay model, we see the next stage with a HA Viva made in fibreglass. Whether this view represents a 'final design', a styling development of the car, or its next stage in life as the HB Viva, we have no idea. However, a clue may well be gained from the pictures on the walls around the car, as these look very much like the embryo HB model. It is, therefore, likely that both these pictures refer to the metamorphism of the Viva, rather than its genesis, but whatever the case, the original HA Viva design concept would have started off in life like this; designs, sketches, mock-ups, wooden models, clay models, fibreglass shells and finally completed cars. Much more work would then follow in the Engineering Department before the model was ever put on general release!

Another essential requirement for the new saloon, was the potential to develop into car-derived commercial vehicles. Light vans, pick-up trucks and small estate cars were all planned around the 1,057cc four-cylinder engine. This strong little engine had a large bore and a short stroke, a down-draught single Solex carburettor, and produced 44bhp giving a top speed of around 80mph. Transmission was by an all synchromesh four-speed gearbox, using a short floor-mounted gear stick. This gave much faster changes through the gears, and thus made it ideal for new drivers!

Originally just the basic and Deluxe saloons were offered, which were offered respectively at £527 7s 11d and £566 1s 3d including Purchase Tax. Without this tax the cars cost £436 and £468. This meant the government was collecting around £100 in tax for each car produced, which wasn't a bad return on its financial assistance when one considers that 100,000 Vivas had been sold within 10 months of the car's launch — that was a cool £10 million in going back into the Chancellor's coffers. The fairly solid Labour votes from the car workers employed at the plant wouldn't have harmed Harold Wilson (himself a Merseyside MP) or his new government either.

Even the basic Viva offered spacious accommodation for four passengers, but it was a bit pinched with five adults. The boot offered quite a good 10cu ft of load space, achieved by the square boxy shape of the car. However, some of the reviewers of the time failed to appreciate that Vauxhall was actually promoting a low-cost entry point for the new motorist, and criticised the car as being 'Spartan'.

Heaven forbid anyone should criticise, and for Alan Earnshaw the Viva was certainly a step up from the BSA, Ariel or Triumph motorbikes and the draughty sidecars that he had had to endure on family trips to the seaside. Huddersfield to Scarborough or Blackpool in one uncle's basic Viva was far better than the same journey in another uncle's motorcycle combination. Anyway, to resolve the criticisms Vauxhall did introduce a better-appointed SL saloon ready for the summer of 1965.

The Viva's dimensions were an overall length of 12ft 11in x 4ft 11in x 4ft 5in high. The turning circle was 29ft 6in. They were painted in a new 'Magic Mirror' acrylic lacquer paint, and came in a choice of Grecian White, Storm Grey, Meteor Blue or Calypso Red. The Deluxe came in the same basic colours, but also black, Pacific Blue, Jade Green or Cavalry Fawn.

The SL and SL90 Viva models, with their more luxurious appointments, featured a colour scheme with a contrasting flash along their sides that was surrounded by a chrome border. In all some 11,794 SL and SL90s were built, but this was a tiny figure compared with the other 309,538 Viva saloons that were built before the HB Viva was introduced in 1966.

In August 1964 the HA range was expanded with a car-derived six-cwt van, the first such car-based light commercial produced by Vauxhall since the PC Bedford van had been phased out in favour of the 10-/12cwt CA in 1952. This was later offered as an eight-cwt van, and finally in the 10cwt capacity in 1972 to cater for the increasing loads that small commercials were expected to carry. Coverage of the HA van is not appropriate in this present volume, but two passenger-carrying derivatives of the van must be considered.

As mentioned earlier, there was one member of the Viva family that was not particularly well known in the UK, namely the Epic. This was primarily an export version of the HA Viva, and it was built both in Luton and at the Liége plant in Belgium, and pictured here in a publicity picture taken in a snowy Scandinavian setting.

The Viva got its name from a fellow Yorkshireman. This particular Yorkshireman was one William Swallow, who became Vauxhall's Managing Director in 1961. It fell to him to chose a name that suited the little car, and the one that he eventually devised conjured quite a bit of Latin flare. The Viva name carried on through various series in the Vauxhall range until 1979 when the HC Viva was phased out — meantime around 1.6 million cars wore Swallow's Viva badge!

The bright mouldings on the side show this to be a HA Viva Deluxe. It is powered by a 1,057cc engine based on its German cousin, the Opel Kadett.

The Martin Walter prototype HA Dormobile seen here in February 1965. Although the Viva, the Beagle and their light commercial equivalents shared many identical components, not everything was the same. One example would be the van doors, which looked like those on the car but were actually taller; another major difference was the gearbox and prop shaft.

Above: The attraction of a light commercial van, which could also double as a family saloon, was a well-tried concept by the time that the HA came along. Ford with its 100E series, Austin (with the A35 Countryman) and Morris (with the 1000 Traveller) had shown this to be quite a lucrative market — especially with the small businessman or commercial traveller. This internal view of the HA shows the load-space area with rear seat down, with period electrical equipment in the back and Vauxhall photographer Norman Page in the front.

Left: Another market for the Beagle was found in both agricultural circles. As this picture seems to suggest, this 1,057cc estate was quite capable of carrying milk churns (presumably if the milk tanker forgot to call), or for going shopping in!

From the outset the new HA van body could be purchased with rear side windows, and one issue of the *Bedford Magazine* showed how an electrical company had created illuminated adverts to fit behind the 'glass panels', but the idea never really caught on. What did take off was the rather attractive 'estate car' version of the HA, which was known as the Bedford Beagle. This was in production from 1963 to 1967, and it was often sold for a dual role: a commercial vehicle during the day and a family saloon in the evenings or weekends.

By 1965 the firm of Martin Walter was busily converting the Bedford CA chassis into a very practical camper. With the arrival of the HA van, it found it could offer a smaller Dormobile model. Fitted with an elevating roof and called the Roma, the small Dormobile was equipped to carry two adults and a child. However, it also had an awning that could be fitted to provide extended accommodation when the tailgate was in the open position. The Roma filled a very interesting niche in the market, being the first modern camper van aimed primarily at married couples rather than family groups.

Alan Earnshaw vividly remembered walking through the town centre of Holmfirth one Saturday in 1964 on his way to play football at school. Here a young local musician named Roy Castle was playing his trumpet and tap dancing in front of a display stand. The event was to attract attention to the arrival of the new Vauxhall HA Viva, and the whole town seemed to be examining this popular little car. Here we see a picture of what Vauxhall envisaged as one of its popular roles — the small family saloon. This is an early HA built at the firm's Ellesmere Port plant in Cheshire. It was one of the 307,738 HA Vivas built before the company introduced the HB Viva in 1966.

PB VELOX AND CRESTA 1962-1965

After the wonderful, ostentatious and (to a degree) extravagant PA series Velox and Cresta, many commentators expressed surprise at the unveiling of the PB range that succeeded them. The launch of the new range of six-cylinder cars showed that Vauxhall was now offering a large, but quite orthodox looking saloon. The only thing that the PA and PB series had visually in common was the Velox and Cresta names. Again the Cresta was furnished with the lion's share of extra equipment, but it cost around £100 more than the Velox.

In appearance the two new large cars had a lot of family resemblance to the smaller FB model Victor. True, the Velox and the Cresta had a much more 'gutsy' look about them. Whereas the Victor had gentle, soft flowing lines to the bonnet and boot, the Velox and the Cresta had a defined edge to theirs.

The Victor's boot also had an attractive curve, but the six-cylinder models had a pronounced chamfer to their counterbalanced boot. Just below the lid, horizontal lamp clusters were mounted in a lozenge-shaped housing. Both cars had fine chrome work, and a notable feature was the rear bumper, which had a central recess to accommodate the number plate. On the Cresta a fine chrome band ran along the top corner of the rear wings, crossed the doors, then passed along the front wings to finish at a peak in the wing a few inches above the headlamps.

The headlamps themselves were set outside the radiator grille, which was made up from a series of horizontal chrome bars and one singular vertical band in the centre. Another feature, the sidelight and indicator cluster, is readily seen from the picture below. Mounted in the bottom of the wing, just above the bumper, they were more readily observed by other road users. Vauxhall described these as an improved safety feature, which they were, but as the cars aged they were badly affected by mud and debris that was thrown up from the road. If this built up behind them and caused rusting, and in the case of a good friend (who shall remain nameless) it cost him a couple of points on his licence. When travelling down the cobbled Alder Street, in Huddersfield late at night, the nearside cluster in his 11-year-old Velox, dropped free — unfortunately he was following a police car at the time.

The cars were 15ft 1in long and were carried on Firestone 5.90 x 14in tubeless tyres. They were powered by six-in-line engines of a square configuration, which had an 82.6mm bore and stroke that gave a displacement of 2,651cc. They were also fitted with a single Zenith 42VNT carburettor. This continued the Vauxhall reputation for producing a powerful saloon, and again the six-cylinder cars were used in a large number of competitions, including the Monte Carlo Rally, but it was as a top flight family saloon or businessman's car that they really excelled.

A manual three-speed gearbox was the standard option, but automatic transmission was provided with the Hydra-Matic gearbox that was available as an 'optional extra' on either car. Interestingly, in addition to the normal park, neutral, drive, and low positions on standard automatic gearboxes, the Hydra-Matic had a further position marked 'S'. When this position was selected it held the second gear up to a maximum speed of 59mph and changed down at 52mph. Overdrive was also available as an option!

Suspension on the new PB cars was by independent coil springs and wishbones, with telescopic dampers at the front and half-elliptic leaf springs and automatic dampers at the rear. The brakes were Lockheed hydraulic with vacuum servo assistance, with disc brakes at the front and drum brakes at the rear.

Around four-and-a-half miles south of Hungerford on the A338 road, an early PB Velox reaches the crossroads of the Marlborough road. The sylvan surroundings of the Berkshire countryside, the quiet road, and the lovely old road sign bring back memories of days when vehicles were individual and a journey was a great adventure!

This view captures a little recorded aspect of daily life in Vauxhall's works at Luton, with cars coming off the end of the production line. Here we see the final inspection process being undertaken on a batch of early PB Velox and PB Cresta models before their delivery to the dealers or despatch to the docks for export. The many checks that were undertaken here were quite essential, as they ensured that the final quality of the build met the standards set down by the company.

Full six-seater comfort and their powerful six-cylinder engines help explain why the PB Vauxhall models were well liked by taxi operators. In many ways the Vauxhall PB range proved to be very practical taxis and hire cars, offering a degree of luxury at a reasonable price. Quite a number were also used by firms operating funeral services and wedding cars. It is not surprising therefore that black was one of the standard paint schemes offered by Vauxhall, what is more it should be noted that a number of firms also offered a hearse conversion to the six-cylinder Vauxhalls.

This picture clearly illustrates the external changes that were incorporated in the top car within the PB range. This executive model, known as The Radford Cresta, was an official conversion undertaken by the London- based coachbuilders Harold Radford, and was marketed to well- heeled members of the general public between October 1963 and 1964. (Some were also produced for military use as 'staff cars', and a batch were still being exported to the Middle-East as late as the spring of 1965). The exterior of the Radford car was finished in a special paint, and at the rear it featured a silver panel between the taillights. A full folding sunroof, bumper over-riders, dual headlamps and a new style of wheel trim were all featured in the 'extra' appointments of the PB Radford. However, it was the lavish interior where the car showed its 'executive' flair, not least in the glass 'chauffeur's screen' between the front and rear seats. Rear seat passengers enjoyed luxurious extras such as reading lamps.

As mentioned previously, the Cresta was very well equipped, and featured a deep padded top to the facia panel, with a Burr Walnut band embellishing both it and the glove-box locker below. A clock was mounted between the padded sun visors, and even the steering wheel had a padded cross bar. Other refinements included a chrome horn ring on the steering wheel, map pockets in the front foot wells on either side of the car, provision for seat belts, and a powerful heater/demister unit.

Externally the Cresta was identified by the extra chrome trim and by the provision of fog and spot lamps. The Cresta was easily recognised at a distance due to the fact that it was offered in one of six two-tone colour schemes and by the thin white wall tyres it wore.

Improvements were made to the PB range in 1964 when a 3.3-litre engine was fitted to both models, giving 128hp. A floor-mounted four-speed gear change became available as an optional extra, but the most visual change was the introduction of a new full-width radiator grille. Also in 1964 Vauxhall were able to offer estate car versions of the PB Velox and Cresta by Martin Walter. As will be recalled, this Folkestone-based company had begun converting the E-Type Velox in 1957, and it would also go on to be chosen for the conversion to the PC range when introduced in 1965. Yet this seemed a strange decision in light of the fact that the company had already begun a production line build of a Victor estate at Luton.

The Velox was launched with a price of £822 for the standard saloon or £955 for the Hydra-Matic, The standard Cresta cost £919 and £1,052 for the Hydra-Matic, The PB range remained in production for a relatively short time, as the Velox was withdrawn at the end of 1964, and the PB Cresta superseded by the PC Cresta in the summer of 1965. Yet in the short period of time they were in production, a total of 87,047 cars were produced, and this outstripped the 81,841 of the PA Velox and Cresta models, and almost reached the massive total of 91,923 cars produced in the PASX Velox/PADX Cresta range that the PB Cresta/Velox replaced.

However, their brief lifespan may well have been due to the fact that they were nowhere near as visually appealing as the PA models that had preceded them. In a confidential memo sent to Vauxhall dealers in February 1964, ahead of the PB refinements of that year, the company was promising that a new, exciting six-cylinder car was already under development for launch the following year. The motoring press began to circulate rumours that a new space age car was being promised by Vauxhall, and confidential preview brochures released late in 1964 showed that a radically improved and more stylish car using the 3,294cc power unit was just around the corner. This was to be the PC series, and although it falls outside the remit of this book's time span, we do spend some time covering these cars at the end of the book, as its development definitely falls within the period under discussion.

A 1965 article in the motoring press that asked 'Did Vauxhall Get It Wrong?', alluding to the styling of the PB series, which suggested that a luxury car should not have had a basic styling that could be found on the mid-range family car like the FB Victor. Mind you, to take that argument a step forward, if you looked closely enough, you could even see a distinct likeness to the front end of the boxy little HA Viva.

The fact that Ford had changed from its extremely stylish Consul Classic to the Cortina suggests that there was a certain vogue for the boxy approach in the early 1960s, but was this for the better? For this writer at least, the PB really had lost a great deal of ground that had been captured by the PAs, which had set Vauxhall so far apart from the other six-cylinder luxury cars then being made in Britain. Probably the most reasonable comment on the subject was made by *Classic & Sportscar* in a 1993 supplement, which kindly described the PB range as a 'reskinned six (which) looks like an overgrown FB Victor'.

Mind you this was still in a time that anything produced at Luton sold, and sold in large quantities to boot. The change from public transport to private car ownership had grown out of all proportion to the national economic growth, but it undoubtedly had a great deal to do with the massive reduction in public transport, in a period when the infamous Dr Richard Beeching wielded his 'Axe' and decimated British Railways. In the year following his report, 1964, Vauxhall achieved its all-time high of 342,873 vehicles, an aggregate of 6,500 cars a week. Perhaps these figures speak for themselves, and suggest that the PB was just another step on the road to raising the standard!

One part of the PB range that had a really stylish appearance, was the Martin Walter estate car conversion, which looked just like a production model. In itself this suggests that there was little wrong with the PB's front-end appearance, and that it was basically the back end that was at fault. By contrast the back end of the estate suggested a certain harmony that was not achieved on the earlier six-cylinder estate conversions (where the back end looked very much like an after-thought). The long association between Vauxhall/Bedford and the Folkestone firm of Martin Walter is part of a unique story, and one that needs much deeper consideration. As will be appreciated from this book, the story goes back quite a way and carried on not only through the estate car conversions, but also on Dormobile crew buses, 'camper vans' and ambulances based on the CA chassis. Yet Martin Walter did much more, and the Vauxhall archive contains many unusual prototype pictures with Martin Walter bodies on Luton-built chassis. Included in these views are pictures of a school bus based on the Bedford VAS chassis.

Showing a distinct improvement on the FB Victor range, the new FC series looked a much more stylish car than its predecessor. This view shows the style of the anodised aluminium radiator grill on the 1964-1966 Victor 101, before it was re-designed in September 1966. The FCD Victor 101 Super was sold at a price of £708 when it was first introduced in saloon car form in October 1964.

FC VICTOR 101 AND VX/490 1964-1967

Although we are now approaching the cut-off date for this book, the company introduced two important models just before the end of 1964. Although several of the vehicles featured in the pages that follow actually postdate 1964, the models themselves are an integral part of our story. The first of these was the Vauxhall Victor 101FC, which was introduced in October 1964 to replace the FB Victor. It was available in two body shells, offering either a four-door saloon or a five-door estate. The range of models offered on these two types was much wider, and in total six different cars were available. The range started with a basic saloon (the FCS), which was launched with a £678 price tag. For this modest price you got a four-door family saloon in a choice of six body colours, with seating for four to five passengers on front and rear bench seats.

The upholstery used on the basic model was Vynide (horribly sticky stuff on a hot sunny day), and the floor had the luxury of fitted rubber mats (which were slippery in wet weather). These appointments were complimented by a single sun visor for the driver, a single-tone horn and column gear change. Mind you, if you wanted to splash out on an optional extra or two you could get individual front seats and a floor-mounted gear stick. If you had £708 to spend, you could move up a step to the FCD, otherwise known as the Super Saloon.

This was slightly better appointed than the basic model, and had bright-work in the form of anodised aluminium strips. Inside the floors were carpeted, whilst the facia panel was covered in a padded material. Courtesy lights were another luxury, and these were automatically operated by switches in the doors. Oh, and by the way, the front seat passenger could now put away their sunglasses, as a second visor was provided. There was a choice of nine single-tone body colours.

The Victor 101 Deluxe (code FCE) benefited from even more refinement, most noticeably the upholstery, which used a material called Ambla. If this wasn't enough, you could get leather furnishing as an optional extra. The bench seat — standard on the other models — was replaced by two thickly padded single seats on the Deluxe version. Armrests were fitted to the doors, and beneath the thick cut-pile carpet a sound insulating material was fitted to the floor. A heater-defroster, windscreen washer, dual horns and twin sun visors all came as standard. Externally new wheel embellishers and chrome hubcaps were fitted and drip mouldings were made from anodised aluminium. Floor-mounted gear change was available, but as an optional extra. The Deluxe cost just £763 and came in a choice of seven single- or five two-tone colours. These two-tone colours were applied in the same way as the early PA Cresta saloons, with the second colour being applied to the roof panel and luggage compartment.

The sum of £775 bought you a very practical estate car — the FCW — that had a 51.6cu ft of load space. The dimension of the cargo area was 69in x 53½in with the rear seats folded down. A one-piece, top-hinged tailgate with counter-balanced torsion beams, provided a wide entry aperture. This was a useful feature that endeared the estate to several police forces and ambulance services. Equipment was the same as the Super saloon, but the Super estate version was also available in a choice of four two-tone shades. A second estate car — the FCG — carried the name Victor Deluxe Estate, and had the luxurious appointments of the Deluxe saloon. It came in six single-tone colours and four two-tone shades and carried the 1964 price of £859. The sixth and final car in the range was the superb VX4/90 saloon. Offering higher performance from its 1,595cc four-cylinder engine, the VX4/90 developed 85.5bhp in twin carburettor form. A four-speed gearbox was fitted as standard, but 'Power-Glide' automatic transmission became an option on all Victor models in May 1965. A slight fault in the VX4/90 led to a number of prematurely worn clutches and, as a consequence, Vauxhall redesigned the clutch housing and began fitting these in October 1965. Retrospective fitting was carried out by the dealerships on cars in service, if the owners reported a problem, but not everybody experienced trouble. At the same time the air filter was replaced, following a redesign to cope with below par performance. The VX4/90 had several features that set it apart from the other models sharing the same body shell. The first was the stylish radiator grille and the side flash in a contrasting colour to the body paint. The VX4/90 carried its own distinctive badge, initially fitted on the off-side corner of the boot lid, this was later moved to a far more prominent position on front wings. As I recall, the badge was also something of a collector's item by unscrupulous schoolboys with screwdrivers.

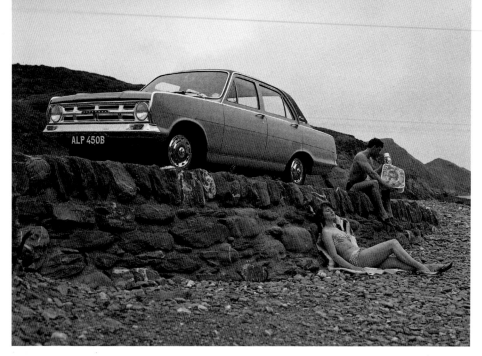

This car was the prototype FC Vauxhall VX4/90, and it featured in a large number of publicity pictures ranging from mountain locations to 'beach shots'. It will be seen that the prototype does not have a side flash, which was a feature of the production model, and it has a different coloured roof panel but this does not appear on the production models. The car was registered in London partially to disguise the fact it was a prototype, as it attracted less attention than a Luton registration.

Internally the VX4/90 was the most luxurious of the FC models, and consequently this gave it the edge over many of its contemporaries. A test report in *The Motor* magazine commented: 'the quality of a Rover or Wolseley at the price of a Ford.' Unlike the other models in the range, where a four-speed gearbox was only an option, on the VX4/90 it came as standard with a floor-mounted gear lever.

The dashboard also had a different instrument panel and facia, with a four-cowled circular instrument panel (this was up-dated by means of a polished walnut-effect finish from 1966 onwards). Because of the advantageous price (when compared to contemporary cars of a similar type), the VX4/90 found itself being adopted by several police forces. Naturally it did well with those forces that already had an allegiance to the Vauxhall marque, but it also sold to many new ones as well.

Progressive improvements were made on the flagship of the range until the FC was replaced by the overhead cam engined models of the FD series in August 1967.

In August 1965 a different numbering system was adopted by Vauxhall, and this affected all the Victor models. The following year saw a new anodised aluminium grille being fitted across the range, and the addition of bright sill moulding below the doors of the Deluxe models. Other improvements included re-designed seating and improved interior trim, and bigger front brake cylinders. A nagging problem with water penetration in some cars was resolved by improved weather-strip sealing and a substantial development in the technology used to make the glass screens. The estate cars also benefited from the fitting of larger wheels and tyres, and this alleviated several road-handling problems that drivers had reported on the earlier models when they were driven fully loaded in poor conditions.

Modest price increases were natural during the life of the FC Victors, but given that this was a time of financial instability in Britain, the cost of the cars did not keep up to the level of inflation. There was therefore a gradual reduction in the real price of the FC range over the period, a factor that was achieved by Vauxhall's continual investment in modern manufacturing facilities. By the time that the series came to its end in August

Like the six-cylinder PC range, the four-cylinder FC models benefited from an increased cabin space as a result of the pronounced curvature of the doors and window glass. This added internal space gave much more comfortable accommodation for four passengers, and it wasn't all that cramped when five adults were carried.

Comparisons of the production line VX4/90 (above) and the prototype (ALP 450B) seen below. The pictures show the stylish lines of one of the new high-performance six-cylinder cars. It will be noted that the production model also carries the new side flash, but this is missing from the prototype. The prototype was actually given individual front seats, a floor-mounted gear change on a four-speed gearbox, and a new facia panel with different instrumentation for the instruments. The difference this made in the driving of the car, was instantly recognised and with variations the revised layout was applied to the production line VX4/90s. These cars also featured a four-dial instrument package that looked quite impressive. This package included a water/oil-pressure gauge, a tachometer, a speedometer (with mileage recorder and trip meter), and an ammeter (with ignition, generator and indicator direction lights). The car seen in the upper picture (taken outside the prestigious Park Lane Hotel), can be readily identified as one of the earlier production models by the fact that the VX4/90 badge is positioned on the rear window pillar, but this was later positioned on the rear wings instead.

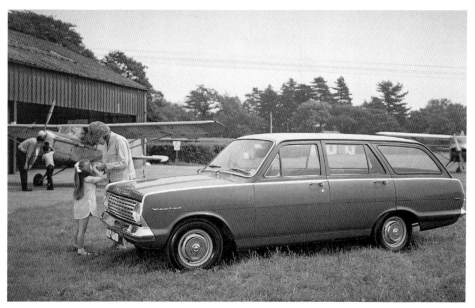

Versatile in either the role of a comfortable family saloon car, or as a two-seat load carrier offering 51.7cu ft capacity, the FCW Victor 101 was an exceptionally versatile car. The estate was available in any one of five single tone colours, or one of four two-tone body colours as shown here. From these pictures it will be noted that the second colour was basically applied to the roof panel, and the upper half of the real tailgate.

Showing the dividing line in the two colours, this picture gives a fascinating rear-three-quarter view and well illustrates its spacious nature. With its pleasing proportions the estate had an overall length of 174.7in, and as much as 69in of length within the load space compartment. This was quite enough room to accommodate a chest of drawers, bags of animal feed and several bales of hay.

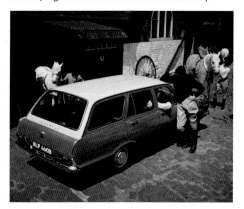

1967, the basic FCS saloon cost £721, whilst the Super was listed as £771 and the Deluxe at £807. The estate versions cost £847 and £911, and the VX4/90 £927. Taking the basic car as an example, we see that the price had actually increased by £43 but the model purchased in 1967 was a substantial improvement on that introduced three years earlier.

That the FC Victor provided a range of popular saloon cars and estates can be demonstrated by the production figure between October 1964 and August 1967, as 219,814 Victors and 13,449 VX4/90s were produced before the FD series was launched.

PC CRESTA AND VISCOUNT 1965-1972

Although the PC range really belongs in the next part of the Vauxhall story, its inclusion in the book covering the period 1945-1964 is really quite essential, for it shows the substantial change in the range from the offerings of the post-war period. Advertised with the slogan 'The Cars For The Space Age', the new Vauxhall PC Cresta and Cresta Deluxe officially replaced the PB Cresta and Velox on 18 October 1965, a time when the Velox name was finally dropped. However, as their genesis, and most of the research and development work, took place in 1964, it is appropriate to include the PC in this book. It was also the last variant in a long line of Vauxhall cars to carry the Cresta badge. Whereas the PAs had seen a production figure of 173,364, the demand dropped with the PBs to 87,047 and, despite a seven-year production line, the PCs would only total 60,937 when production ended in 1972. The high demand for large powerful cars was coming to an end in Britain, especially in 1967 after the Middle East conflict in June (resulting in high petrol prices), the imposition of the 70mph speed limit in July and the devaluation of the pound in the autumn.

The new six-cylinder cars came to be known for the 'Coke-bottle style', so-called because of the way in which the wing line rose towards the rear in imitation of the distinctive glass bottles used for the well-known fizzy drink. It was a popular feature, and its public appeal led to Vauxhall emulating the feature on the FB Victor and the FD Victor.

The demise of the Velox meant that there were two Cresta models, the PCS being the base model, whilst the PCD was the designation for the Deluxe. Later the 140bhp Viscount would appear, but as it did not come on the scene until the summer of 1966, it is well and truly beyond the remit of this book. However, all three models shared a single body-shell and had the same mechanical layout.

Once again examination of Vauxhall's publicity records show that the company were aiming some of their products at very specific markets. One of the markets it identified for its estate car products was the 'country set', and many of the pictures show estate cars on farms, race-courses, stables, golf courses, grouse shoots and so on. Another set of photographs showed the estates on airfields, giving the impression it was the car for the 'Jet Set'. Here we see a 'farm setting' for a 1964 Victor FC Model 101 Super Estate. Interior space on the FC models was improved by using curved side windows. The model remained in production until 1967.

The heart of the beast was the powerful 3.3 litre six-in-line engine, however this unit could be traced back quite a way, for it had originally been designed by Chevrolet to power light trucks. In its more modern form it had been used in the 1964-5 PB Velox and Cresta cars, where it brought about the unique situation of being the first Vauxhall car that was not powered by a Vauxhall-designed engine. The advantage of taking the American engine for the PB can be readily understood, when its 128bhp compared favourably against the 113bhp 2.6 litre engine used in the PAs and early PBs. The new engine had a cylinder bore of 92.08mm diameter and 82.55 stroke giving 3,294cc. One criticism of the engine might be expressed in that it only had a four-bearing crankshaft, but otherwise it was a marvellous piece of machinery.

However, alternatives were provided as optional extras. The first of these gave an overdrive variant, operating on the top two ratios after activation by a toggle switch. The next option was a four-speed manual box with a floor-mounted column, which gave a much quicker passage through the gears. The third, and my favourite was the Powerglide automatic box, and whilst not everyone's cup of tea, it has to be admitted that this really was a superb piece of engineering. I have read some critical reports of the Powerglide, but I can do no better than echo Vauxhall's own description of what they called 'the world's best proved automatic transmission.' Indeed, it changed gear with a smoothness that could not be felt, and I did quite a lot of work with Vauxhall and the Powerglide in my days at Browns. I also know that several UK motor manufacturers secretly had the unit to bits including Rolls Royce, who (reputedly) used the Powerglide's successor, namely the General Motors Overseas Operations automatic gearbox.

Superior, superb, superlative, were all words that Vauxhall used to describe the new PC Cresta and PC Cresta Deluxe when it was introduced in 1965. As can be seen from the below picture it was clearly a car aimed at the businessman (or those who wanted a car of quality and comfort), and its ability for high-speed cruising mirrored this.

As this car, registered in the States Of Jersey, shows the Deluxe Cresta had a timeless grace and elegance. David Jones' styling was right for the mid-1960s, but it still looks good today, and it would also compare favourably with any small limousine in the years between. It was a car well ahead of its time, and it worked wonders to overcome the lack-lustre appearance of the PB range that preceded it.

Another PR shot that suggests a certain style in the six-cylinder Vauxhall, and as the BOAC pilot strides out towards a pre-production model Viscount, the suggestion is made that here is a car that accords with a certain status in life. After all, the man who 'drives' the most luxurious aircraft in the world had to have a car commensurate with his position! Didn't he?

If the engine and transmission had American origins, the body had a real Luton pedigree, for it was styled by David Jones ARCA. Jones had joined Vauxhall from the Royal College of Art. When he arrived in 1934, he was the styling department, but it was not too long before he received an assistant. By the time that the PC range was on the drawing board, a new £2.5 million Styling & Engineering Department had opened in 1964. We have to say that the styling of the PC series did much to restore 'image confidence' in the Vauxhall range, following the less than kind comments that some had made about the FB and PB series cars. In the PC range, Jones went on to produce a car style that matched the power unit and automatic transmission, and after the initial success with Cresta, Vauxhall could send out a sumptuous brochure on 20 April 1966. With this the Sales Manager (G E Moore) announced the arrival of a 'high prestige car which combines great refinement and luxury with a really exciting performance'. The price was £1,457 12s 11d.

Hydraulic brakes with vacuum-servo assistance were fitted on the front wheels which had 10$\frac{1}{2}$in diameter discs, whilst the rear wheels used nine-inch diameter drum brakes. The wheels were usually shod (at least for the home market) with 5.90 x 14 tubeless cross-ply tyres, although special 7.00 x 14 four-ply nylon tyres were available for the driver who wanted sustained high-speed motoring without the need for frequent adjustment of tyre pressures. Externally the base Cresta was easily identified by its individual seven-inch diameter headlamps, whilst the Deluxe version sported dual headlamps of 5$\frac{3}{4}$in diameter. The radiator

This is a left-hand drive Deluxe model. Despite its Swiss registration plate, this shot was taken at Gayhurst near Milton Keynes.

grilles on the two models showed a slight difference, whilst the Deluxe also had a small and very discreet badge at the edge of the bonnet, whereas the base model just had a narrow name badge. Other small differences could be seen in the trim. Whilst both cars had bright trim around the panoramic front and rear windscreens and on the side drip rail around the windows, the Deluxe also had a fine band running along the base of the side windows which then carried on along the top of the rear wings.

Compared with the PB, the PC was a handsome-looking automobile from any perception, yet its styling was also very practical. By the clever use of curved doors and side glass, Vauxhall was able to construct a car that was a good half-inch narrower than its predecessors, and at the same time give an extra four inches of width within the car saloon. Overall the PC was 69^4/sin wide, and its length was 181^4/sin on a 107^1/2in wheelbase and resulted in the PC being some 5^3/10in longer overall. This, coupled with a change in the position of the petrol tank (from over the rear axle to a position underneath the boot floor), gave a slight rise in the height of the boot. These two factors provided an increase of 16.07cu ft in the luggage space over the PB models, and increased the PCs to 30cu ft.

Further examples of Vauxhall's continued improvement were to be found in the internal specifications. To suit their limousine status, the Deluxe Crestas were given a better heater/ventilation system. This not only provided a good floor heater and screen demister, but also incorporated small grilles at the outer ends of the facia panel that gave cool air distribution at face level. The floor heater directed air to each front foot well, and two more ducts directed heat into the two rear seat foot wells. This heater system was also available on the base Cresta, but only as an additional cost item.

A close study of the PC will reveal how much thought had gone into its design during 1963 and 1964, and less obvious features were the high quality of sound insulation and the 44% increase in overall rigidity. 'Underfloor Comfort' (now there's a concept to think about) began to appear in Vauxhall technical literature, so it is worth briefly discussing. On the PC, Solbit Deadener spray was applied to the internal floor and transmission tunnel, and the Deluxe also had Flinkcote pads front and rear. Both models had ^{5}/8in jute felt matting covering the front and rear floor panels, with a further ^{3}/8in strip covering the transmission tunnel. A final layer of ^{3}/8in Polyether was placed on the rear floor before the carpets were fitted. On the underside of the Deluxe models floor panels, a substantive layer of under-sealant was applied.

In its seating accommodation the Cresta offered a new luxury soft fabric called Ambla on the Deluxe model, but still stuck with Vynide, which was still awful on a hot sunny day. Leather remained an optional extra on both models. The Deluxe had individual front seats as standard, but a bench seat with centre armrest was available as an extra. The base model stuck to the bench seat, but a centre armrest was again supplied as extra equipment. Both models had armrests as standard in the rear seats. The quality facia incorporated a large instrument panel, and all the standard item controls. It could also be fitted with additional equipment such as an electric clock, a built-in radio, fog lamp switch, rear window demister control, and a steering wheel lock on the ignition switch. The 10 'Magic Mirror' paint finishes for the Cresta were black, Grecian White, Storm Grey, Kestrel Grey, Meteor Blue, Pacific Blue, Cypress Green, Calypso Red, Cavalry Fawn and Jade Green. Interior colours were Calypso Red, Delta Blue, April Green and Grey Beige, in monotone finishes on the Cresta and two-tone trims on the Deluxe.

The PC concludes our look at the 20 years of Vauxhall development following the end of World War 2. Our consideration of the subject has, hopefully, put this all into context and shown the progression through the years. It has not been intended as an in depth analysis of the subject, but rather an Informative overview of the subject.

The approach is a personal view from the authors, and any mistakes in the text are ours alone, but we have to emphasise that this book would not have been possible without the kind assistance of Vauxhall Motors, numerous Vauxhall enthusiasts and several Vauxhall dealers. The support of Ron Atkins and the Vauxhall Heritage Services team in developing this concept must also be recognised, for without their help, this series of books would simply not have happened.

The clean lines of the PC can be seen on this publicity picture that was used in a 1965 brochure to convey an image of speed. The slight blurring of the image certainly achieves this aim, but we chose this picture for the nice way in which it shows the 'Coke-bottle' styling.

This 1965 Vauxhall Cresta PC saloon is the basic model as the deluxe model boasted dual headlamps. This car featured what was called 'Coke Bottle' styling, and this was carried on to the FD Victor, which replaced the FC101.

Index